Action, Property and Beauty

What are the challenges and potential of complex and emergent urban systems? This book answers this question by shedding new light on the topics of emergence, complexity, and self-organisation and showing their interconnectedness with other concepts, such as property and beauty, which are usually considered separately. It contributes to the discussion by interpreting and explaining the nature of emergent urban phenomena and suggesting more appropriate design and planning measures.

The book explores and untangles these crucial topics in a compact and accessible way by offering fresh interdisciplinary perspectives on the themes of action and interaction, self-organisation, property, neighbourhood adaptability, urban beauty, and suitable public planning and design interventions. It provides novel and crucial insights for students, researchers, and academics in Urban Studies, Planning Theory, Planning Ethics, Planning Law, Legal, Political and Human Geography, Urban and Regional Economics, Urban Sociology, and Urban Design. It is essential for anyone interested in exploring the emergent dynamics of complex urban contexts, as well as for those involved in developing various projects and measures who aim to consider the spontaneous nature of cities seriously.

Stefano Cozzolino is Senior Researcher at ILS – Research Institute for Regional and Urban Development (Dortmund) – and Lecturer at RWTH University (Aachen). His main research interest focuses on the interplay between planning/design and spontaneous social-spatial configurations. He is the coordinator of the AESOP thematic group on Ethics, Values and Planning.

Stefano Moroni is Professor of Planning at Milan Polytechnic University (Italy). He is member of the editorial board of the journal *Planning Theory* and one of the founders of the research network "NormaCtivity: Research Network on Human and Non-Human Normativity". His main research interests are: planning theory; applied ethics; theory and philosophy of the law.

Action, Property and Beauty

Planning with and for Emergent Urban Complexity

Stefano Cozzolino and Stefano Moroni

LONDON AND NEW YORK

First published 2025
by Routledge
4 Park Square, Milton Park, Abingdon, Oxon OX14 4RN

and by Routledge
605 Third Avenue, New York, NY 10158

Routledge is an imprint of the Taylor & Francis Group, an informa business

British Library Cataloguing in Publication Data
A catalogue record for this book is available from the British Library

ISBN: 9781032586892 (hbk)
ISBN: 9781032593388 (pbk)
ISBN: 9781003454304 (ebk)

DOI: 10.4324/9781003454304

Typeset in Times New Roman
by Taylor & Francis Books

Contents

Illustrations

Figures

Tables

1 Introduction

The challenge of urban emergence and complexity

The primary aim of this book is to shed new light on the crucial topics of *emergence, complexity*, and *self-organisation*, and to show their interconnectedness with other concepts, like *property* and *beauty*, that are usually considered separately. The intention is both to contribute to the interpretation and explanation of urban phenomena and to suggest how to more appropriately intervene in them, via design and planning.

A fundamental starting point for the discussion conducted in this book is the difference between *physical-material systems* (e.g. a system of gas particles) and *social systems* (e.g. social-spatial systems like cities). While in physical-material systems the main "components" are simple and non-intentional entities (e.g. atoms), in social systems the "components" are active, self-determining and intentional agents (in a city, for instance, landowners, developers, households, tenants, shopkeepers, etc.) (Portugali, 2012a; 2012b).

Action is therefore the crucial, basic element of complex systems like cities. Action is understood here as the purposeful behaviour of agents who pursue specific ideas and plans in order to achieve a desired state of affairs.[1] Due to its goal-driven nature, action is obviously *intentional*. However, the *interaction* among many independent actions (e.g. multiple, various interactions occurring over time in an urban context) often generates *unintentional* and *unintended* effects (Moroni, 2012; 2018).

Some (i.e. a sub-class) of these unintentional, unintended effects are global *emergent phenomena*. Emergence is that particular relationship between two (or more) elements or aspects whereby one arises out of the other and yet remains distinct from and irreducible to it (Lawson, 1997). Emergent properties imply a "discontinuity" between initial actions (and interactions) and their final product (Archer, 2010).[2] In short, "emergence is a process where larger regularities or patterns

DOI: 10.4324/9781003454304-1

arise through nonlinear interactions among the humans or agents that themselves do not exhibit such properties" (Huang, 2015: 6).[3] Therefore, the idea of real emergence requires a conception of multiple strata or levels of reality.[4] To conclude, *emergent properties* stand in contrast to *aggregate properties*: emergent phenomena depend on their constituent parts but are irreducible to them (Polanyi, 1958; Popper, 1972).[5]

A spontaneous *spatial configuration* (e.g. the way in which buildings and spaces are arranged in an incrementally evolved neighbourhood) may be a simple example of an emerging phenomenon. A *self-coordinating social order* (e.g. the market for raw materials and equipment for pizzerias, pizza restaurants, and pizza consumers) is a more sophisticated example of an emerging system.

It is important to stress (Hua, 2012) that not all *emerging* phenomena are *self-coordinating* systems: that is, emergent patterns of actions which generate systemic expectations that in turn influence and dynamically coordinate the actions and interactions of numerous individuals within that system.[6] In other words, all self-coordinating social systems are emergent but the reverse is not the case. Note that the term "spontaneous order" (introduced by Polanyi, 1951 and Hayek, 1960, 1967) denotes only and specifically self-coordinating (emerging) systems.

Emergent self-coordinating systems in this sense are generally more *complex* and *adaptable* than top-down designed systems.[7] This is because the latter strictly depend on the limited knowledge and skills of those who conceived them at a specific time, while the former are the open and emerging cumulative outcome of the interaction among many actors' minds and abilities over a long time period.

Note that well-functioning emergent systems (for example, well-functioning self-coordinating systems) are not generated in the absence of appropriate *conditions*, for instance adequate *framework rules* (Rauws et al., 2020). Therefore, emergence and self-coordination in social systems are not synonymous with an "absence of rules" or of any "designed coordination" (Moroni, 2011). However, we suggest that the role of designers and planners should be quite diverse and more circumscribed than it is in current practice if we recognise in truly radical terms the emergent properties of cities deriving from action and interaction. In particular, two points must be taken into account. The first of them is that cities are shaped by forces – actions and interactions – that are virtually impossible to control in their entirety. This means that it is possible to govern only a limited part of a city's overall development, and never its details. Second, it is inherently impossible to pre-define an optimal city shape, because the problems and challenges of a city change over time. As a result, it is not possible to anticipate and plan the finest spatial configurations.

From this perspective, complex, emerging cities cannot be efficient in an engineering sense. As Jane Jacobs (1969: 86) provocatively observes: "I do not mean that cities are economically valuable in spite of their inefficiency and impracticality but rather because they are inefficient and impractical". In fact, cities continue to survive and prosper mainly because they work as incubators of new ideas and activities which entail experimentation, trial and error, and innovations (Ikeda, 2023).

Thus, before one tries to intervene in social-spatial systems, it is crucial to understand their functioning, and then work *with* – not *against* – their emerging features.

This book explores and discusses the above synthetised frame with particular attention paid to action and interaction (Chapter 2), self-organisation (Chapter 3), property (Chapter 4), neighbourhood adaptability (Chapter 5), urban beauty (Chapter 6), and public planning and design measures (Chapter 7). A case-study is included as an Annex in order to investigate some crucial aspects of these topics in an empirical context.

This book reworks in a substantial manner – and further develop – some ideas and materials anticipated in previous publications.[8]

Notes

1 Action is crucial in defining an agent as an entity that "does something as opposed to other natural entities to which we attribute no specific actions except metaphorically (e.g. "The sun rises"). In other words, an agent is a source of activity" (Barandiaran et al., 2009: 370).

2 However, emergent properties are "relational" in the sense that they are not contained in the "floor level" elements, but could not exist apart (and independently) from them (Archer, 2010).

3 In this regard, Vesterby (2008: 3) observes: "There are two basic meanings for the term emergent, (a) to come into view or awareness, visually or conceptually, or (b) to come into existence. [...] The first meaning has anthropocentric aspects, while the other does not. Confounding the two meanings has led to a great confusion". In this book the term is always used in the latter sense.

4 On this, see Lewis (2011, 2012). Therefore, real emergence rejects "actualism" (i.e. the view according to which the real is fully reducible to the actual) (Lawson, 1997).

5 On the crucial issue of emergent phenomena and properties, see also Corning (2002), Goldspink and Kay (2004), Johnson (2006), Schenk (2006), Paperin et al. (2011); Kwapień and Drożdż (2012), Lichtenstein (2016), Allen et al. (2018), Artime and De Domenico (2022), Venkatasubramanian et al. (2022), Leong (2023).

6 In this case, a process of "synchronisation" (Strogatz, 2003) occurs without being intentionally organised by anybody.

7 As Lichtenstein (2016: 44) writes: "Emergence increases the *capacity* of the system". And he adds: "The emergent reflects a new way of organizing that dramatically increases the capacity – effectiveness [and] quality – of the system" (Lichtenstein, 2016: 46).

8 For Chapter 2, see: S. Moroni, S. Cozzolino, S., Action and the city: Emergence, complexity, planning, *Cities*, 2019, 90: 42–51 (DOI: 10.1016/j.cities.2019.01.039); for Chapter 3: S. Moroni, W. Rauws, S. Cozzolino, Forms of self-organisation: Urban complexity and planning implications, *Environment and Planning B*, 2020, 47(2): 220–234 (DOI: 10.1177/2399808319857721); for Chapter 4: S. Cozzolino, S. Moroni, Multiple agents and self-organisation in complex cities: The crucial role of several property, *Land Use Policy*, 2021, 103: 1–7 (DOI: 10.1016/j.landusepol.2021.105297); for Chapter 5: S. Cozzolino, The (anti) adaptive neighbourhoods. Embracing complexity and distribution of design control in the ordinary built environment, *Environment and Planning B*, 2020, 47(2): 203–219 (DOI: 10.1177/2399808319857451); for Chapter 6: S. Cozzolino, On the spontaneous beauty of cities: Neither design nor chaos. *Urban Design International*, 2021, 27: 43–52 (DOI: 10.1057/s41289–021–00170-w); S. Cozzolino, A crisis of lost values: rediscovering the relationship between urban beauty, democracy, and complexity, in J. Portugali (ed.) *The Crisis of Democracy in the Age of Cities*, Cheltenham: Edward Elgar, 2023, 220–245 (DOI:10.4337/9781803923055.00022); for Chapter 7: S. Cozzolino, S. Moroni, Structural preconditions for adaptive urban areas: Framework rules, several property and the range of possible actions, *Cities*, 2022, 130: 1–7 (DOI: 10.1016/j.cities.2022.103978); S. Moroni, S., Cozzolino, Conditions of actions in complex social-spatial systems, in G. de Roo, C. Yamu, C. Zuidema (eds.), *Handbook on Planning and Complexity*, Cheltenham: Edward Elgar, 2020, 186–202 (DOI /10.4337/9781786439185.00014); S. Moroni, S. Cozzolino, S., Action and the city: Emergence, complexity, planning, *Cities*, 2019, 90: 42–51 (DOI: 10.1016/j.cities.2019.01.039); for the Annex: S. Cozzolino, Planning and design for long-term neighborhood adaptability: an investigation of the formation and evolution of Kreuzviertel in Dortmund, Germany. Urban Design International (Forthcoming; DOI: 10.1057/s41289-024-00243-6).

References

Allen, T.F., Austin, P., Giampietro, M., Kovacic, Z., Ramly, E., Tainter, J. (2018). Mapping degrees of complexity, complicatedness, and emergent complexity. *Ecological Complexity*, 35: 39–44.

Archer, M.S. (2010). Morphognenesis versus structuration: On combining structure and action. *The British Journal of Sociology*, 61: 225–252.

Artime, O., De Domenico, M. (2022). From the origin of life to pandemics: Emergent phenomena in complex systems. *Philosophical Transactions of the Royal Society A*, 380: 1–21.

Barandiaran, X.E., Di Paolo, E., Rohde, R. (2009). Defining agency: Individuality, normativity, asymmetry, and spatio-temporality in action. *Adaptive Behaviour*, 17 (5): 367–386.

Corning, P.A. (2002). The re-emergence of "emergence": A venerable concept in search of a theory. *Complexity*, 7 (6): 18–30.
Goldspink, C., Kay, R. (2004). Bridging the micro-macro divide: A new basis for social science. *Human Relations*, 57 (5): 597–618.
Hayek, F.A. (1960). *The Constitution of Liberty.* Chicago: Chicago University Press.
Hayek, F.A. (1967). *Studies in Philosophy, Politics and Economics.* London: Routledge.
Hua, H. (2012). Planning meets self-organization: Integrating interactive evolutionary computation with cellular automata for urban planning. *Frontiers of Architectural Research*, 1 (4): 400–404.
Huang, J.P. (2015). Experimental econophysics: Complexity, self-organization, and emergent properties. *Physics Reports*, 564: 1–55.
Ikeda, S. (2023). *A City Cannot be a Work of Art.* Singapore: Palgrave-MacMillan.
Jacobs, J. (1969). *The Economy of Cities.* New York: Vintage Books.
Johnson, C.W. (2006). What are emergent properties and how do they affect the engineering of complex systems? *Reliability Engineering & System Safety*, 91 (12): 1475–1481.
Kwapień, J., Drożdż, S. (2012). Physical approach to complex systems. *Physics Reports*, 515 (3-4): 115–226.
Lawson, T. (1997). *Economics and Reality.* London: Routledge.
Leong, D. (2023). Action in complexity: Entanglement and emergent order in entrepreneurship. *The Journal of Entrepreneurship*, 32 (1): 182–217.
Lewis, P. (2011). Varieties of emergence: Minds, markets and novelty. *Studies in Emergent Order*, 4: 170–192.
Lewis, P. (2012). Emergent properties in the work of Friedrich Hayek. *Journal of Economic Behavior & Organization*, 82: 368–378.
Lichtenstein, B. (2016). Emergence and emergents in entrepreneurship: Complexity science insights into new venture creation. *Entrepreneurship Research Journal*, 6 (1): 43–52.
Moroni, S. (2011). Land-use regulation for the creative city. In D.E. Andersson, A.E. Andersson, C. Mellander (eds), *Handbook of Creative Cities.* Cheltenham: Edward Elgar, 343–364.
Moroni, S. (2012). Land-use planning and the question of unintended consequences. In D.E. Andersson (ed.), *The Spatial Market Process.* Bingley: Emerald, 265–288.
Moroni, S. (2018). Individual motivations, emergent complexity and the just city: Is egoism one of the main problems of contemporary social-spatial realities, and altruism the principal antidote? *Cities*, 75: 81–89.
Paperin, G., Green, D.G., Sadedin, S. (2011). Dual-phase evolution in complex adaptive systems. *Journal of the Royal Society Interface*, 8 (58): 609–629.
Polanyi, M. (1951). *The Logic of Liberty.* London: Routledge.
Polanyi, M. (1958). *Personal Knowledge.* London: Routledge.

Popper, K.R. (1972). *Objective Knowledge.* Oxford: Clarendon Press.

Portugali, J. (2012a). Complexity theories of cities: Achievements, criticism and potentials. In: Portugali, J., Meyer, H., Stolk, E. (eds) *Complexity Theories of Cities Have Come of Age.* Berlin: Springer, 47–62.

Portugali, J. (2012b). Complexity theories of cities: First, second or third culture of planning?. In: De Roo, G., Hillier, J., Van Wezemael, J. (eds) *Complexity and Planning*. Farnham: Ashgate, 117–140.

Rauws, W., Cozzolino, S., Moroni, S. (2020). Framework rules for self-organizing cities: Introduction. *Environment and Planning B*, 47 (2): 195–202.

Schenk, K.E. (2006). Complexity of economic structures and emergent properties. *Journal of Evolutionary Economics*, 16 (3): 231–253.

Strogatz, S. (2003). *Sync: How Order Emerges from Chaos in the Universe, Nature, and Daily Life.* New York: Hyperion.

Venkatasubramanian, V., Sivaram, A., Das, L. (2022). A unified theory of emergent equilibrium phenomena in active and passive matter. *Computers & Chemical Engineering*, 164: 1–12.

Vesterby, V. (2008). *Origins of Self-organization: Emergence and Cause.* Goodyear, AZ: ISCE.

2 Action

1 Introduction

Since Jane Jacobs' (1961) pioneering, ground-breaking work, cities have increasingly come to be seen as complex systems. This has had a certain impact on descriptions and explanations of urban phenomena (e.g. Batty, 2007), but far less on the issue of planning regulations and measures.[1] In short, a serious consideration of the issue of complexity poses entirely new challenges for planning; challenges which demand new responses.[2] In order to delve deeper into these issues, this chapter will consider a fundamental question (often taken for granted, but far from obvious): Why is a city actually complex? Answering this question will help in reconsidering (throughout the entire book) another crucial issue – this too anything but trivial or banal: What is the possible and desirable role of planning in complex cities?

2 Focus: Why the city is complex

The complexity of cities does not depend solely on the fact that they are made up of many components; their complexity is due mainly to the fact that the core element of cities is multiple *action*. As Juval Portugali (2016: 4) observes: "As a set of material components alone, the city is an artifact and as such a simple system; as a set of human components the urban agents the city is a complex system". John Habraken (1998: 7) stresses the same point: if a built environment is a complex entity, "it is so by virtue of human actions: people imbue it with life". In brief, agents transform the city into a complex system: actions are unquestionably the main source of its complexity.

This chapter therefore assumes (human) action to be a crucial aspect of urban complexity. Yet it makes a distinction between (i) individual actions and (ii) the interaction between them. This

DOI: 10.4324/9781003454304-2

distinction introduces relevant descriptive aspects regarding, for instance, the nature of complex urban dynamics; but it also highlights a number of key issues that must be taken into account by planners who wish to tackle city complexity.[3]

The term "action", as the starting point of our discussion, seems preferable to "behaviour" because it averts the reductionist fallacy of behaviourism (Werlen, 1993); that is, the reduction of human agency to the mere stimuli-response model. Observe that the term "action" seems also preferable to the term "decision", as traditionally used by certain orthodox neoclassical economics, because the term action suggests more a process than an instantaneous operation; a process which also involves social interaction (de Soto, 2008: 1–2). In the large part of orthodox neoclassical economics, agents are effectively treated as if they must merely decide what to do:

> To make such decisions, the agent is considered to have certain data about its economic environment available (e.g., prices, interest rates), obtained at no cost to itself […]. A different way to say all this is that agents do not interact directly with one another in neoclassical models.
>
> (Axtell, 2007: 109)[4]

3 Discussion: Action and interaction

This section explores and discusses the role of action and interaction in creating complex urban systems.

3.1 First issue: Action

Three features are crucial in defining urban action: (i) *intentionality*, (ii) *subjectivity*, and (iii) *uncertainty*.

First of all, human action is defined here as the purposeful behaviour of agents who implement specific plans in order to achieve a certain desired state of affairs. Action takes place at present and is directed toward the future satisfaction of an aim; if the entirety of an individual's desires could be instantaneously realised, the reason for acting would immediately disappear (Rothbard, 1997: 59). Through action, agents attempt to shape their environment according to their will, desires and needs. Agents in a city – landowners, developers, households, shopkeepers, members of associations and so on – are active actors, who erect new buildings, adapt existing ones, open businesses, repurpose disused areas, create new services. They are engaged in and operating for the attainment of specific objectives that they consider worth pursuing. Observe that all action is in the first place an individual action: only an individual can actually adopt a conception of a desirable life, make choices in light of this and act accordingly (Mises, 1963). Saying this does not imply that distinct individuals cannot jointly act, in groups, for the same cause or intent (e.g. to start a new urban business, a new cohousing scheme or an energy community[5]); the point is simply that the *source* of action, including collective action, is inevitably the individual.[6] Nor does saying this imply that society is interpreted as "atomistic": as demonstrated below, all actions are interconnected and give rise to emergent phenomena that are "more than the mere sum of their parts". Observe also that agents, including economic agents, are not necessarily conceptualised here as selfish. Action is based on purposefulness but not necessarily on any selfishness of purpose (Kirzner, 1992). Action is actually a process of applying means to *whatever ends* an individual may choose: an agent can adopt any ends he/she likes (Rothbard, 1970/2004: 1322).[7] Observe, to conclude, that action is undertaken by some specific actors for some specific purpose at a certain *time* and *place*; in short, actions are always a matter of real time and real space.[8]

Second, actions are the expression of subjectivity and, consequently, of the inexorable diversity of agents' values, needs and preferences. In short, individuals do not behave "objectively"; they are not passive operators and responders, but agents actively engaged in subjective choices (Buchanan, 1982: 69). In fact, actions imply choices made by individuals who not only perceive and interpret the world differently, but also have different ideas about what makes life worth living. Cities in this respect are typically places where different, sometimes conflicting, lifestyles, interests and values are intermingled. As Jane Jacobs puts it (1961: 241), cities are inevitably "the creation of incredible numbers of different people [...] with vastly differing ideas and purposes".

Third, actions inevitably interfere, to different degrees, with the course of urban events; that is, they imply changes at some point. The main motivation for starting to act is the expectation that certain activity will re-direct the course of events toward the desired outcome. It should be therefore noted[9] that the concept of action itself logically implies the fact of uncertainty concerning the future.[10] If our actions do not alter the course of events, we have no real choice; if we do indeed have real choices, and our choices do alter the course of events, it is impossible to ascertain in detail what effects such actions have, since our actions interrupt that course (Koslowski, 1990; Callahan, 2002).

Two specifications are required before continuing.

The first specification concerns the role of *knowledge*. Any action takes place within certain conditions, and employs certain means.[11] However, it is human cognition and knowledge that make means valuable or not: certain natural elements, for instance, only become "resources" through human knowledge and agency.[12] Of importance here is not only *theoretical knowledge* but also *practical knowledge*. Such practical knowledge is contextual and dispersed among all individuals; it is "know-how" as opposed to "know-that" (Hayek, 1948). Observe that it is not simply a form of local knowledge, but a contextual, situated one (i.e. tied to a personal experience of time and place); and it is not simply a form of unexpressed knowledge, but strictly speaking a tacit, inarticulate, one (i.e. a type of knowledge that is internalised in the mind of individuals, who make use of it without any awareness: Polanyi, 1966). Its distinctiveness stems from the fact that no single body of expertise can replace this kind of practical knowledge: it remains inevitably dispersed among individuals and cannot be directly collected and concentrated in one single mind.[13] The non-direct accessibility of this form of dispersed social knowledge – which plays a fundamental role in the functioning of cities – creates a severe problem for orthodox, technocratic forms of planning.[14] Even traditional forms of communicative planning cannot overcome this obstacle.[15] As Friedrich von Hayek (1948) pointed out, individuals can indirectly, unwittingly and unpremeditatedly share dispersed practical knowledge by taking part in collective forms of interaction over time (e.g. market exchanges) and thanks to certain devices (e.g. the price system or other impersonal devices).

The second specification concerns the notion of *agency*. Some recent studies tend to grant agency not only to humans but also to objects and things: they speak of "agency of things" and "material agency".[16] They do so in the wake of some well-known works by Bruno Latour (2005). However stimulating and challenging this perspective may be, we believe that it is not entirely acceptable. In other words, we certainly can and must also include things and objects in our image of the world (not only as means but also as conditions for human action: Moroni and Cozzolino, 2020),[17] and even try to make objects and technologies smarter and more interactive (Rathore et al., 2016); but this does not automatically entail recognising a real form of agency to things. In fact, if *human agency* is defined (as done above and seems unavoidable) as the capacity to intentionally form and pursue one's own aims and if *material agency* is defined as "the capacity for non-human entities to act on their own, apart from human intervention" (Leonardi, 2011: 148), or "the things technology can do that are not entirely under the control of users" (Leonardi, 2013: 70), then the term "agency" has a different meaning in the two cases. Matters do not change if material agency is defined – as sometimes happens – in a partially different way: for example, as the ability of objects to exert some influence on human behaviour, or as the ability of objects to react in some way to human behaviour. We therefore prefer to speak more properly of *agency* only when (human) *purposefulness* is at stake.[18] This is also in the belief that going too far in eliminating distinctions between human entities and non-human entities generates logical paradoxes.[19]

3.2 Second issue: Interaction

Three points are crucial in discussing interaction between multiple urban actions: (i) *unintentionality*, (ii) *emergence* and (iii) *unpredictability*.

First of all, it is important to stress that the emphasis on action as intentional and purposeful behaviour does not imply that cities as a whole are or can be the intended results of predetermined rational objectives. The aspect of intentionality implicit in the concept of action in fact should not be wrongly interpreted as meaning that all the consequences of an action are expressly intended by some agent. If this were the case, the psychological sciences alone would suffice to account for any social-spatial phenomenon, like the city.[20] In practice, in a complex world actions can have intentional effects but are likely to come with unintentional results as well. While the outcome of a particular individual action is previously planned and intentionally addressed, in complex systems, such as the city, how other agents will react to it cannot be known in advance. In complex systems, a large part of the social environment of any adaptive agent is represented by numerous other adaptive agents; therefore, a significant portion of any agent's efforts to adapt is devoted to adapting to other adaptive actions (Holland, 1995: 10).

Secondly, it is important to stress that the final result of such processes is therefore more likely to be *emergent* than the outcome of a rational construct. In particular, processes of this kind in cities can give rise to unplanned patterns beyond the boundaries of human design (Ikeda, 2017). In other words, emergence is a key characteristic of complex social-spatial systems. Emergence can be defined as the cumulative result, over time, of countless actions, but not as the direct outcome of a single design (Figure 2.1). Nevertheless, it is reductive to see emergence simply as an "aggregation" of actions. Rather, emergence can give rise to systemic and interconnected wholes. Consequently, emergence in cities is not necessarily synonymous with chaos or disorder but is instead something that can provide a series of collectively recognisable patterns which in their turn foster social interaction and enable the coordination of multiple actors. This process, namely self-organisation (or, better, self-coordination as will be better clarified in Chapter 3), concerns the spontaneous emergence of order at a global level from a vast number of self-reinforcing interactions at the local level without any form of central coordination. Rather than being planned by exogenous forces, self-organisation is the result of enduring interactions among multiple and various agents' plans that structure social relationships (Alfasi and Portugali, 2007: 167).

Emergence does not produce only social structures. Its effect is also observable in cities' material configurations, as a result of multiple concrete actions over time. Typical examples are the "organic" morphological patterns that have emerged without rigid city plans,[21] the hidden logic of the built environment or the different local building types.[22]

In short, actions in complex systems are inevitably parts of an interrelated whole that brings about the emergence of global patterns. The fact that emergent orders and patterns are based on the dispersed knowledge of agents implies that they cannot be artificially designed,

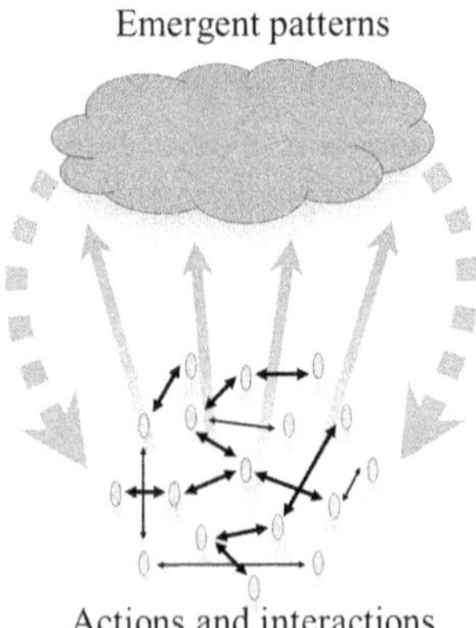

Figure 2.1 Actions, interactions and emergence

nor mechanically reproduced. Actually, emergence consists of a non-reductionist process where simple actions and reactions by the component parts of a system give rise to complex patterns of order which are beyond the capacity of each of the components to create; these patterns are even too complex for them to be grasped at first sight (Pennington, 2002a: 57).

Thirdly, the *specific* outcome of this interaction among many separate actions is, by definition, unpredictable. Any urban action has immediate effects, to some extent intentional and predictable, along with remote side-effects, which are not necessarily intended or predictable because they depend on interaction with others. By acting, we intentionally bring about certain things, while unexpectedly provoking other things and chain reactions (Moroni, 2012). This kind of unpredictable process characterises the dynamic of complex cities. This does not mean that it is impossible to foresee anything; it implies only that *specific predictions* are impossible and that we must be content with *qualitative predictions.*[23] According to Hayek (1967), a "specific prediction" is one able to predict certain discrete events with a sufficient degree of precision; by contrast, a "qualitative prediction" does not predict particular events at all, but only peculiarly wide classes of events; it can solely indicate of what kind the expected event might be.

Two specifications are necessary before concluding.

Firstly, it is important to stress that the issue of the emergence of structures and formation of patterns can be grasped through qualitative-sociological approaches,[24] but also through more formalised models, such as the so-called agent-based models, now applied also to urban issues.[25] The use of formalised models is obviously welcome in the urban realm, provided that one is content to provide an *explanation of the principle* and not an *explanation of detail.* In parallel with the above discussion of prediction (see Table 2.1), we have an explanation of detail when we are able to explain single events and processes; by contrast, we have an explanation of the principle when we are only able to explain typical kinds of events and processes: for instance, types of patterns that arise when certain general conditions are satisfied (Hayek, 1967). The impossibility of providing an explanation of detail of a system like the city depends, among other things, on the structural fact that the creativity of human action is an intrinsic part of the urban system (and, therefore, technological, organisational, managerial innovations: Sayer, 1979). It is often thought that the knowledge generated by our models is helpful in guiding planning decisions directly. Instead, the real usefulness of models of this kind is, in many cases, that they clarify what we *cannot know* or what we *cannot do.* As Hayek (1967: 16) observes on discussing models that provide explanations of the principle: "Such models are valuable on their own, irrespective of their use for determining particular situations, and even where we know that we shall never have the information which would make this possible". In short, the understanding of the general mechanism which produces patterns of a certain kind is not "a tool for specific predictions but important in its own right", and sometimes provides "indications of the desirability of no action" (Hayek, 1967: 40). In the planning literature, Juval Portugali (1999) clearly and appropriately warned against a strictly engineering use of (new) models.[26]

Secondly, it is important to stress that not all emergent phenomena or patterns are here assumed as inherently good or desirable. For instance, certain emergent patterns can be broadly considered as positive (e.g. the clustering of valuable economic activities driving the regeneration of a formerly run-down neighbourhood) while others can be regarded as negative (e.g. the overcrowding of certain built-areas with the risk of encountering hygiene and health issues). It is interesting to note that not even Hayek, one of the staunchest supporters of the importance of spontaneous emergent phenomena, ever claimed that they are always and all desirable (Vanberg, 1994). What really matters here is grasping the *nature* of these processes and seeing whether and how planning can effectively work with them (Bertaud, 2018). In other words, we do not claim that any emerging order is good in itself (or always preferable to other types of designed orders). Nevertheless, we acknowledge that most urban phenomena are inevitably the product of processes of this kind. In short, emergence in complex cities is unavoidable and there are good reasons for planners to relate productively to it.

In conclusion, all the foregoing discussion of action and interaction can be summarised in Table 2.2.

Table 2.1 Explanation and prediction of urban processes in simple and complex systems

	Type of explanation	*Type of prediction*
Simple systems	Explanation of detail	Specific prediction
Complex systems	Explanation of the principle	Qualitative prediction

Table 2.2 Main features of human action and interactions

	Main features	
Action	*Intentionality*	Human action is a purposeful behaviour of agents who implement specific plans in order to achieve a specific desired state of affairs
	Subjectivity	Human action is the expression of the inexorable diversity of agents' values, preferences and capacities
	Uncertainty	The concept of human action implies uncertainty concerning the future; it inevitably interferes with the course of urban events
Interaction	*Unintentionality*	Global effects of interaction are for the large part unintended
	Emergence	Interaction gives rise to unplanned patterns beyond the boundaries of human design
	Unpredictability	Specific predictions are impossible (predictions are limited to wide classes of events).

4 Conclusion

This chapter has underlined the importance of directing the attention of urban studies and planning theory to *action* as the real driver and constitutive basis of what we call "city". The complexity of the city depends, in fact, not simply on the multiplicity of individuals who live in it, but above all on the fact that these individuals ceaselessly *act* and *interact*.

In light of what has been said thus far, the classic criticism of technocratic planning that it forgets *people* seems correct, but partial. What orthodox technocratic planning – and often, in reality, other forms of planning – above all forget are the *actions* (of people); that is, not so much the fact that people living in the city have personal interests and needs (i.e. they are the bearers of interests and needs), but the fact that they *act* actively and adaptively to satisfy them.

Recognising the complexity of cities and the self-organising character of social-spatial systems based on multiple actions and interactions does not necessarily mean rejecting the idea of having public planning policies and measures; nor does it mean welcoming visions of an urbanism "beyond the State" (Savini, 2017). Rather, it implies the recognition of a different – neither marginal nor irrelevant – role of public authorities in providing certain conditions that can effectively deal with complexity and self-organisation without forgoing their potential. The point here is not "public regulation and intervention" *versus* "laissez-faire", but "public regulation and intervention of one kind" *versus* "public regulation and intervention of another kind".[27]

A complex, self-organising urban order based on action and interaction is accordingly not an anarchic one; rather it is an order that needs certain kinds of public rules and infrastructures (Chapter 7). From this perspective, there is no necessary contradiction between defending public regulation and intervention and welcoming complexity and self-organising forces (Cozzolino et al., 2017).

Notes

1 As underscored by Innes and Booher (2010), Wilkinson (2012), Moroni (2015).
2 As highlighted e.g. by De Roo (2000); De Roo and Silva (2010); Giezen et al. (2015); Boelens and De Roo (2016); Partanen (2016); Rauws and De Roo (2016); Sengupta et al. (2016); Talen (2016); Rauws (2017).
3 What we shall say about action, interaction and complexity is influenced by the approach of the Austrian school of economics (as evidenced by the following references to some of its best-known historical exponents, Mises and Hayek, until recent developments, e.g. Kirzner). This will bring out a particular conception of complexity not necessarily superimposable *in toto* on other schools of thought on urban complexity. On the distinctiveness of the Austrian approach to complexity, see the discussions by Kilpatrick (2001), Montgomery (2000), Koppl (2010) and Rosser (2010 and 2012).
4 Obviously, more complex and interactive concepts of what a decision is (e.g. Simon, 1959) would be more compatible with the approach adopted here.
5 See e.g. Moroni (2014); De Franco et al. (2023).
6 See again Mises (1963). As he writes: "All actions are performed by individuals. A collective operates always through the intermediary of one or several individuals whose actions are related to the collective as the secondary source" Mises (1963/1998: 42).
7 For more on this issue (with specific reference to urban systems), see Moroni (2018).
8 See Ikeda (2012). See also O'Driscoll and Rizzo (1985) and Andersson (2005).
9 On this, see especially Mises (1963), Langlois and Everett (1992) and Wubben (1995).
10 On uncertainty in this sense, see e.g. Moroni and Chiffi (2021, 2022); Chiffi et al. (2022).
11 We can speak of *conditions of action* in the case of those aspects of a situation that are not under the direct control of the actor (i.e. those elements that he/she cannot modify), and of *means* for those elements that

can be controlled by the actor (i.e. those elements that he/she can modify) (Parsons, 1937).

12 On this crucial point, see Simon (1996), Kirzner (2000), Reisman (2002), Bauer (2004), Kebir and Crevoisier (2008).

13 See, with specific reference to urban contexts, Ikeda (2004, 2007, 2012).

14 See Pasour (1991); Pennington (2003); Moroni (2019).

15 The participatory/communicative approach is too much focused on a form of communication that is mainly conscious, explicit, verbal and face-to-face, and is therefore insensitive to forms of communication that are unconscious, tacit, extra-linguistic and remote – such as the price mechanism that acts in the market like a telecommunication system, taking into account the large body of social knowledge which cannot be put in words (Pennington, 2002b and 2004).

16 See e.g. Knappett and Malafouris (2008), Buser (2014); Caronia and Cooren (2014); Cruickshank and Trivedi (2017); McGraw and Krátký (2017).

17 For recent studies on this issue, see Lorini et al. (2021, 2023), Lorini and Moroni (2022).

18 It may be that future developments in artificial intelligence will change matters radically. But, at the moment, these are completely futuristic/ speculative hypotheses. On the other hand, if it is *real* artificial intelligence, would we still talk of "agency *of things*" or "*material* agency"?

19 See Krause (2011), Chandler (2013), Bargetz (2018), Häkli (2018). As Krause (2011: 3010) observes, what inanimate objects clearly lack "is the reflexive sense of self required for the affirmation of one's subjective existence through concrete action in the world". It is not required nor it is desirable to abandon "the individuated, reflexive, and norm-responsive subjectivity within agency that is so crucial to sustaining [...] the obligations of democratic citizenship" (Krause, 2011: 318).

20 That the explanation of social phenomena cannot be reduced to psychological issues *precisely because of the unintentional effects of individual actions* was clearly underscored by Hayek (1952), Popper (1945) and Watkins (1968).

21 On this, see e.g. Vance (1990), Kostof (1991), Hamouche (2004), Nilufer (2004), Totry-Fakhoury and Alfasi (2017).

22 On this, see e.g. Akbar (1988), Brand (1995), Habraken (1998), Kropf (2001).

23 Certain scenario building techniques can be interpreted in these terms (Moroni and Chiffi, 2021). For an interesting discussion of the compatibility between a certain scenario approach and the Austrian (Hayekian) epistemology of complexity, see Aligica (2007).

24 See in particular Archer (1995), Lawson (1997), Bhaskar (1998).

25 See e.g. Benenson (1998), Batty (2005), Fossett and Waren (2005), Fontaine and Rounsevell (2009), Jayaprakash et al. (2009), O'Sullivan (2009), Huang et al. (2014), Guo et al. (2019), Marini et al. (2019).

26 For interesting discussions of how agent-based modelling can be usefully employed – in an Austrian (Hayekian) line of thought – see Nell (2010) and Seagren (2011).

27 On this, see e.g. Moroni (2011); Moroni and Minola (2019); Buitelaar et al. (2021).

References

Akbar, J. (1988). *Crisis in the Built Environment.* Singapore: Concept Media Pte Ltd.

Alfasi, N., Portugali, J. (2007). Planning rules for a self-planned city. *Planning Theory*, 6 (2): 164–182.

Aligica, P.D. (2007). Uncertainty, human action and scenarios. *The Review of Austrian Economics*, 20 (4): 293–312.

Andersson, D.E. (2005). The spatial nature of entrepreneurship. *The Quarterly Journal of Austrian Economics*, 8 (2): 21–34.

Archer, M.S. (1995). *Realist Social Theory.* Cambridge: Cambridge University Press.

Axtell, R.L. (2007). What economic agents do: How cognition and interaction lead to emergence and complexity. *The Review of Austrian Economics*, 20 (2–3): 105–122.

Bargetz, B. (2018). Longing for agency: New materialisms' wrestling with despair. *European Journal of Women's Studies*, 26 (2):181–194.

Batty, M. (2005). Agents, cells, and cities: new representational models for simulating multiscale urban dynamics. *Environment and Planning A*, 37 (8): 1373–1394.

Batty, M. (2007). *Cities and Complexity.* Cambridge: The MIT Press.

Bauer, P.T. (2004), *From Subsistence to Exchange and Other Essays.* Princeton: Princeton University Press.

Benenson, I. (1998). Multi-agent simulations of residential dynamics in the city. *Computers, Environment and Urban Systems*, 22 (1): 25–42.

Bertaud, A. (2018). *Order without Design: How Markets Shape Cities.* Cambridge: The MIT Press.

Bhaskar, R. (1998). *The Possibility of Naturalism.* London: Routledge.

Boelens, L., De Roo, G. (2016). Planning of undefined becoming: First encounters of planners beyond the plan. *Planning Theory*, 15 (1): 42–67.

Brand, S. (1995). *How Buildings Learn.* London: Penguin.

Buchanan, J.M. (1982). *The Domain of Subjective Economics.* College Station, TX: Texas A&M University Press.

Buitelaar, E., Moroni, S., De Franco, A. (2021). Building obsolescence in the evolving city. Reframing property vacancy and abandonment in the light of urban dynamics and complexity. *Cities*, 108: 1–7.

Buser, M. (2014). Thinking through non-representational and affective atmospheres in planning theory and practice. *Planning Theory*, 13 (3): 227–243.

Callahan, G. (2002). *Economics for Real People.* Auburn: The Mises Institute.

Caronia, L., Cooren, F. (2014). Decentering our analytical position: The dialogicity of things. *Discourse & Communication*, 8 (1): 41–61.

Chandler, D. (2013). The world of attachment? The post-humanist challenge to freedom and necessity. *Millennium*, 41 (3): 516–534.

Chiffi, D., Moroni, S., Zanetti, L. (2022). Types of technological innovation in the face of uncertainty. *Philosophy & Technology*, 35 (94):1–17.

Cozzolino, S., Buitelaar, E., Moroni, S., Sorel, N. (2017). Experimenting in urban self-organization. Framework-rules and emerging orders in Oosterwold (Almere, The Netherlands). *Cosmos and Taxis*, 4 (2): 49–59.

Cruickshank, L., Trivedi, N. (2017). When your toaster is a client, how do you design? Going beyond human centred design. *The Design Journal*, 20: 4158–4170.

De Franco, A., Moroni, S., De Lotto, R. (2023). Energy communities in a smart urban ecosystem. Institutional, organizational, psychological, technological issues. In M.M. Sokołowski, A. Visvizi (eds). *The Routledge Handbook of Energy Communities and Smart Cities*. London: Routledge, 13–25.

de Roo, G. (2000). Environmental conflicts in compact cities: complexity, decisionmaking, and policy approaches. *Environment and Planning B*, 27: 151–162.

de Roo, G., Silva, E.A. (eds) (2010). *A Planner's Encounter with Complexity*. Farnham: Ashgate.

de Soto, J.H. (2008). *The Austrian School*. Cheltenham: Edward Elgar.

Fontaine, C.M., Rounsevell, M.D. (2009). An agent-based approach to model future residential pressure on a regional landscape. *Landscape Ecology*, 24 (9): 1237–1254.

Fossett, M., Waren, W. (2005). Overlooked implications of ethnic preferences for residential segregation in agent-based models. *Urban Studies*, 42 (11): 1893–1917.

Giezen, M., Bertolini, L., Salet, W. (2015). Adaptive capacity within a megaproject. *European Planning Studies*, 23 (5): 999–1018.

Guo, C., Buchmann, C.M., Schwarz, N. (2019). Linking urban sprawl and income segregation. Findings from a stylised agent-based model. *Environment and Planning B*, 46 (3): 469–489.

Habraken, N.J. (1998). *The Structure of the Ordinary*. Cambridge, MA: MIT Press.

Häkli, J. (2018). The subject of citizenship. Can there be a posthuman civil society? *Political Geography*, 67: 166–175.

Hamouche, M.B. (2004). The changing morphology of the gulf cities in the age of globalisation: the case of Bahrain. *Habitat International*, 28 (4): 521–540.

Hayek, F.A. (1948). *Individualism and Economic Order*. Chicago, IL: The University of Chicago Press.

Hayek, F.A. (1952). *The Counter-Revolution of Science*. Glencoe: The Free Press.

Hayek, F.A. (1967). *Studies in Philosophy, Politics and Economics*. London: Routledge.

Holland, J. (1995). *Hidden Order*. New York: Basic Books.

Huang, Q., Parker, D.C., Filatova, T., Sun, S. (2014). A review of urban residential choice models using agent-based modeling. *Environment and Planning B*, 41 (4): 661–689.

Ikeda, S. (2004). Urban interventionism and local knowledge. *Review of Austrian Economics*, 17 (2/3): 247–264.

Ikeda, S. (2007). Urbanising economics. *The Review of Austrian Economics*, 20 (4): 213–220.

Ikeda, S. (2012). Entrepreneurship in action space. In D.E. Andersson (ed.), *The Spatial Market Process.* Bingley: Emerald, 105–134.

Ikeda, S. (2017). The city cannot be a work of art. *Cosmos and Taxis*, 4 (2/3): 79–86.

Innes, J.E., Booher, D.E. (2010). *Planning with Complexity.* London: Routledge.

Jacobs, J. (1961). *Death and Life of Great American Cities.* New York: Random House.

Jayaprakash, C., Warren, K., Irwin, E., Chen, K. (2009). The interaction of segregation and suburbanisation in an agent-based model of residential location. *Environment and Planning B*, 36 (6): 989–1007.

Kebir, L., Crevoisier, O. (2008). Cultural resources and regional development. In P. Cooke, L. Lazzaretti (eds), *Creative Cities, Cultural Clusters and Local Economic Development*, Cheltenham: Edward Elgar, 48–69.

Kilpatrick, H.E. (2001). Complexity, spontaneous order and Friedrich Hayek. *Complexity*, 6 (3): 16–20.

Kirzner, I. (1992). *The Meaning of Market Process.* London: Routledge.

Kirzner, I. (2000). *The Driving Force of the Market*. London: Routledge.

Knappett, C., Malafouris, L. (eds) (2008). *Material Agency.* Berlin: Springer.

Koppl, R. (2010). Some epistemological implications of economic complexity. *Journal of Economic Behavior & Organization*, 76 (3): 859–872.

Koslowski, P. (1990). The categorical and ontological presuppositions of Austrian and neoclassical economics. In A. Bosch, P. Koslowski, R. Veit (eds), *General Equilibrium or Market Process.* Tübingen: Mohr, 1–20.

Kostof, S. (1991). *The City Shaped.* London: Thames and Hudson.

Krause, S.R. (2011). Bodies in action: Corporeal agency and democratic politics. *Political Theory*, 39 (3): 299–324.

Kropf, K.S. (2001). Conceptions of change in the built environment. *Urban Morphology*, 5 (1): 29–46.

Langlois, R.N., Everett, M.J. (1992). Complexity, genuine uncertainty, and the economics of organisation. *Human Systems Management*, 11 (2): 67–75.

Latour, B. (2005). *Reassembling the Social.* Oxford: Oxford University Press.

Lawson, T. (1997). *Economics and Reality.* London: Routledge.

Leonardi, P.M. (2011). When flexible routines meet flexible technologies: Affordance, constraint, and the imbrication of human and material agencies. *MIS Quarterly*, 35 (1): 147–167.

Leonardi, P.M. (2013). Theoretical foundations for the study of sociomateriality. *Information and Organisation*, 23 (2): 59–76.

Lorini, G., Moroni, S. (2022). Non-propositional regulation. *Philosophical Investigations*, 45 (4): 512–527.

Lorini, G., Moroni, S., Loddo, O.G. (2021). Deontic artifacts. Investigating the normativity of objects. *Philosophical Explorations*, 24 (2): 185–203.

Lorini, G., Moroni, S., Loddo, O.G. (2023). Regulatory artifacts: Prescribing, constituting, steering. *International Journal for the Semiotics of Law*, 36 (1): 211–225.

Marini, M., Gawlikowska, A.P., Rossi, A., Chokani, N., Klumpner, H., Abhari, R.S. (2019). The impact of future cities on commuting patterns: An agent-based approach. *Environment and Planning B*, 46 (6): 1079–1096.

McGraw, J.J., Krátký, J. (2017). Ritual ecology. *Journal of Material Culture*, 22 (2): 237–257.

Mises, L. (1963). *Human Action*. Auburn, AL: Ludwig von Mises Institute, 1998.

Montgomery, M.R. (2000). Complexity theory. An Austrian perspective. In D. Colander (ed.), *Complexity and the History of Economic Thought*. London: Routledge, 227–240.

Moroni, S. (2011). Land-use regulation for the creative city. In D.E. Andersson, A.E. Andersson, C. Mellander (eds), *Handbook of Creative Cities*. Cheltenham: Edward Elgar, 343–364.

Moroni, S. (2012). Land-use planning and the question of unintended consequences. In D.E. Andersson (ed.), *The Spatial Market Process*. Bingley: Emerald, 265–288.

Moroni S (2014). Towards a general theory of contractual communities. In D. E. Andersson, S. Moroni (eds), *Cities and Private Planning*. Cheltenham: Edward Elgar, 38–65.

Moroni, S. (2015). Complexity and the inherent limits of explanation and prediction. *Planning Theory*, 14 (3): 248–267.

Moroni, S. (2018). Individual motivations, emergent complexity and the just city: Is egoism one of the main problems of contemporary social-spatial realities, and altruism the principal antidote? *Cities*, 75: 81–89.

Moroni, S. (2019). Critically reconsidering orthodox ideas: Planning as teleocratic intervention and planning as a rational decision method. *Planning Theory & Practice*, 20 (3): 323–338.

Moroni, S., Chiffi, D. (2021). Complexity and uncertainty: implications for urban planning. In J. Portugali (ed.), *Handbook on Cities and Complexity*. Cheltenham: Edward Elgar, 319–330.

Moroni, S., Chiffi, D. (2022). Uncertainty and planning: Cities, technologies and public decision-making. *Perspectives on Science*, 30 (2): 237–259.

Moroni, S., Cozzolino, S. (2020). Actions and conditions of actions. In G. de Roo, C. Yamu, C. Zuidema (eds), *Handbook on Planning and Complexity*. Cheltenham: Edward Elgar, 186–202.

Moroni, S., Minola, L. (2019). Unnatural sprawl: Reconsidering public responsibility for suburban development in Italy, and the desirability and possibility of changing the rules of the game. *Land Use Policy*, 86: 104–112.

Nell, G.L. (2010). Competition as market progress: An Austrian rationale for agent-based modeling. *The Review of Austrian Economics*, 23 (2): 127–145.

Nilufer, F. (2004). Hidden morphological order in an organic city. *Protibesh*, 9: 34–41.

O'Driscoll, G.P., Rizzo, M.J. (1985). *The Economics of Time and Ignorance*. London: Routledge.

O'Sullivan, D. (2009). Changing neighborhoods – Neighborhoods changing: A framework for spatially explicit agent-based models of social systems. *Sociological Methods & Research*, 37 (4): 498–530.
Parsons, T. (1937). *The Structure of Social Action*. New York: McGraw-Hill.
Partanen, J. (2016). Liquid planning, wiki-design. *Environment and Planning B*, 43 (6): 997–1018.
Pasour, E.C. (1991). Land-use planning: Implications of the economic calculation debate. In J.C. Wood, R.N. Woods (eds), *Friedrich A. Hayek*, vol. IV. London: Routledge, 1–15.
Pennington, M. (2002a). *Liberating the Land*. London: IEA.
Pennington, M (2002b). A Hayekian liberal critique of collaborative planning. In P. Allmendinger, M. Tewdwr-Jones (eds), *Planning Futures*. London: Routledge, 187–205.
Pennington, M. (2003). Land use planning: Public or private choice. *Economic Affairs*, 23 (2): 10–15.
Pennington, M. (2004). Citizen participation, the knowledge problem and urban land use planning. *The Review of Austrian Economics*, 17 (2): 213–231.
Polanyi, M. (1966). *The Tacit Dimension*. Chicago: University of Chicago Press.
Popper, K.R. (1945). *The Open Society and its Enemies*. London: Routledge.
Portugali, J. (1999). *Self-Organisation and the City*. Berlin: Springer.
Portugali, J. (2016). What makes cities complex? In J. Portugali, E. Stolk (eds), *Complexity, Cognition, Urban Planning and Design*. Berlin: Springer, 3–19.
Rathore, M.M., Ahmad, A., Paul, A., Rho, S. (2016). Urban planning and building smart cities based on the internet of things using big data analytics. *Computer Networks*, 101: 63–80.
Rauws, W. (2017). Embracing uncertainty without abandoning planning. *The Planning Review*, 53 (1): 32–45.
Rauws, W., De Roo, G. (2016). Adaptive planning: Generating conditions for urban adaptability. *Environment and Planning B*, 43 (6): 1052–1074.
Reisman, G. (2002). Environmentalism in the light of Menger and Mises. *The Quarterly Journal of Austrian Economics*, 5 (2): 13–14.
Rosser, B. (2010). How complex are the Austrians? In R. Koppl, S. Horwitz, P. Desrochers (eds), *What is so Austrian about Austrian Economics?* Bingley: Emerald, 165–179.
Rosser, B. (2012). Emergence and complexity in Austrian economics. *Journal of Economic Behavior & Organization*, 81 (1): 122–128.
Rothbard, M. (1970). *Power and the Market*. Menlo Park, CA: Institute for Humane Studies; Auburn: Ludwig von Mises Institute, 2004.
Rothbard, M.N. (1997). *The Logic of Action*. Cheltenham: Edward Elgar.
Savini, F. (2017). Planning, uncertainty and risk: The neoliberal logics of Amsterdam urbanism. *Environment and Planning A*, 49 (4): 857–875.
Sayer, R.A. (1979). Understanding urban models versus understanding cities. *Environment and Planning A*, 11: 853–862.
Seagren, C.W. (2011). Examining social processes with agent-based models. *The Review of Austrian Economics*, 24 (1): 1–17.

Sengupta, U., Rauws, W.S., de Roo, G. (2016). Planning and complexity: Engaging with temporal dynamics, uncertainty and complex adaptive systems. *Environment and Planning B*, 43 (6): 970–974.
Simon, H.A. (1959). Theories of decision-making in economics and behavioral science. *The American Economic Review*, 49 (3): 253–283.
Simon, J.L. (1996). *The Ultimate Resource.* Princeton, NJ: Princeton University Press.
Talen, E. (2016). Planning the emergent and dealing with uncertainty. In T. Haas, K. Olsson (eds), *Emergent Urbanism.* London: Routledge, 141–146.
Totry-Fakhoury M., Alfasi, N. (2017). From abstract principles to specific urban order. *Cities*, 62: 28–40.
Vanberg, V. (1994). J.M. Buchanan, F.A. Hayek: The thought of two Nobel laureates. In P.J. Boettke, D.L. Prychitko (eds), *The Market Process.* Cheltenham: Edward Elgar, 225–228.
Vance, J.E. (1990). *The Continuing City.* Baltimore, MD: Johns Hopkins University Press.
Watkins, J.W.N. (1968). Methodological individualism and social tendencies. In M. Brodbeck (ed.), *Readings in the Philosophy of the Social Sciences.* New York: Macmillan, 269–280.
Werlen, B. (1993). *Society, Action and Space.* London: Routledge.
Wilkinson, C. (2012). Beyond blueprints? Complexity theory as a prospective influence for metropolitan governance. In G. De Roo, J. Hillier, J. Van Wezemael (eds), *Complexity and Planning*. Farnham: Ashgate, 243–268.
Wubben, E. (1995). Austrian economics and uncertainty. In G. Meijer (ed.), *New Perspectives in Austrian Economics.* London: Routledge, 106–145.

3 Self-organisation

1 Introduction

The implications of self-organising phenomena for planning strategies and interventions constitute a relatively new topic of research that is gaining increasing traction with urban planners and in the literature.[1] The problem is that the concept of self-organisation is at present applied in a variety of different ways in the contemporary planning debate, a fact that has generated misunderstandings, dubious definitions, and questionable practical suggestions. As Beitske Boonstra and Ward Rauws (2021: 304) note: "The understanding of self-organisation in urban studies and planning theory is far from uniform".[2]

The aims of this chapter are: first, to unravel this issue by differentiating urban phenomena that are usually all labelled as self-organising; second, to identify which of them is directly connected with complexity and is the most challenging for planning theory and practice.

2 Focus: Different self-organising phenomena

This section presents the features of three different self-organising phenomena which are relevant to the urban realm, and which we shall term: (i) *self-building*, (ii) *self-governance* and (iii) *self-coordination*. In our opinion, clearly distinguishing these types of urban self-organisation is a first and important step toward achieving a critical understanding of the issues at stake.[3]

The three types in consideration here were chosen because they are all generally labelled as "self-organising" urban phenomena in the literature.[4] In effect, all of them have to do with non-hetero-directed forms of organisation, meaning that they are not directly determined from the outside but are instead endogenously generated. While all

DOI: 10.4324/9781003454304-3

three cases have features in common, the tripartition stems from the salient characteristics that differentiate them, as we shall show later.

2.1 First case: Self-organisation as self-building

We use the term "self-building" to denote a situation in which the first occupants arrange for the building of their own homes, participating – to varying degrees and in varying ways – to the production of the housing units (Duncan and Rowe, 1993). In this case, households are directly involved in the production of their homes, rather than buying them ready-built on the market from a traditional developer (Clapham et al., 1993). By "households", here we mean a group of households acting collectively or an individual household acting alone. Their involvement occurs in various ways: (i) households may personally build their home in part or in its entirety, by themselves or with the aid of relatives or friends, for instance (a practice usually termed *self-* or *auto-construction* in a strict sense); (ii) alternatively, they may act as promoters by bringing together the elements of the design, land and construction, even if they are not directly involved in the building process (what can be termed *self-promotion*); (iii) or, lastly, they may be actively involved in programming and managing the building process (*self-development*) (Clapham et al., 1993).

Self-building is therefore a situation in which (future) residents have an active role in the building process of their (future) homes. They truly "have a say" in the building process and the way the end-product is realised and put to use. Self-building implies that the figure of the *initiator* and that of the *user* coincide.[5]

Recently, governments across Europe have attempted to boost self-provided homes. The *Housing Strategy for England*, published in November 2011 by the UK government, includes for instance the objective to encourage and support individuals and groups taking the initiative to build their own homes. In the Netherlands an adjustment of the National *Spatial Planning Act* introduced subsidy schemes for similar reasons.

In short, the main point of self-building is the *enterprising autonomy* of individuals in obtaining their own dwelling. By "enterprising autonomy" we mean the ability of households to undertake their own projects and actions rather than being merely passive consumers of something provided by others.

2.2 Second case: Self-organisation as self-governance

Self-governance involves processes of collective decision-making and action undertaken by groups of people sharing common objectives in relative independence from public actors and institutions. In particular, groups that engage in urban self-governance take responsibility for steering and managing community projects and services which are meant first and foremost to serve their own members (and are only eventually open to other users). In cities, typical examples are homeowner associations, community gardening organisations, and local energy communities.[6] In a homeowner association, for instance, a set of dwelling units are individually owned by the members, and a range of common facilities (streets, parking lots, green areas, etc.) are collectively owned through the association itself. The homeowner association is managed by a board that the members of the association appoint. Members automatically enter the association at the time of purchasing their home. By doing so they also accept a set of basic rules, substantive and procedural, and agree to pay periodic fees for the functioning of the association itself and the management of the common spaces.

Groups that embark on self-governance may vary considerably in size, ranging from very small, closed groups – for instance, a handful of households – to wider community projects involving more people. In all cases, however, members of these groups act and plan their activities voluntarily, while governmental actors remain at a certain distance. In other words, while governments may provide favourable conditions for starting a collective initiative or promote their long-term existence, members of these groups act and plan their moves deliberately in order to achieve a shared goal. Because these organisations have specific, purposeful ends, their members are guided by some form of internal, explicit coordination.

In brief, the main point of urban self-governance is *decision-making independence*. Self-governance is effectively *self-regulation* (i.e. intentionally producing a group's own rules regarding, in our case, the use and transformation of spaces and buildings) plus *self-management* (i.e. intentionally administering and running common services and infrastructures in a certain place) without the direct and substantial guide or support of the public authorities.

2.3 Third case: Self-organisation as self-coordination

Self-coordination can be seen neither as a specific product of deliberate human action nor as a fully natural phenomenon independent from human action. Instead, it entails an emerging process: place-based actions, interactions, and chain reactions produce certain *patterns* in which the expectations and actions of a plurality of agents tend to be spontaneously coordinated. To put it differently, although they are not intentionally organised, emergent patterns of actions generate systemic expectations and orders that in turn influence and coordinate the actions and interactions of numerous individuals within that system (Marshall, 2009).

The variety of actions at the local level and their potential to generate new spontaneous patterns (i.e. self-synchronising supra-individual structures) imply that processes of self-coordination are very difficult to predict in detail. Individuals interact and respond subjectively to their immediate environment in trying to achieve a better fit. As observed in Chapter 2, such responses are based on dispersed knowledge of particular circumstances of time and space.

Examples of emerging self-coordinating mechanisms can be found, for instance, in: real-estate markets and the clustering of economic activities; certain form of urban growth and land-use evolution; traffic patterns and pedestrian flows.[7]

In short, the main point here is *spontaneous alignment*: that is, the process whereby self-synchronisation occurs in society without being intentionally organised by anybody. This process creates a system in which the actions of separate, independent individuals are spontaneously coordinated.

3 Discussion: Challenges

3.1 Similarities and differences among the three types of urban self-organisation

All three types of self-organisation are to a greater or lesser extent part of the urban realm. In this section we discuss their key similarities and key differences (Table 3.1).

Self-building, self-governance, and self-coordination share three key characteristics.

Firstly, all three phenomena represent – and effectively are – forms of organisation of urban activities. Although each does so in different ways, they all introduce a certain *degree of structuration* (e.g. of ordering) into social-spatial situations.

Secondly, and as already mentioned, they are not directed from the outside, in the sense that they do not emerge under the will and guidance of external actors. It is something *endogenous* to them that generates the order in question.

Thirdly, all three self-organising phenomena emerge and develop *relatively independently* of formal public authorities. We say that they are relatively independent – and not completely independent – because they clearly emerge and develop, in their particular and specific form, under certain conditions set by governments. “Relative independence” therefore means here that governments, instead of determining them, posit the institutional background conditions within which the three self-organising phenomena can occur.

In the case of self-building, these institutional conditions include, amongst others, public building standards.

In the case of self-governance, initiatives must take place in accordance with public rules that establish the boundaries within which it can legitimately happen: public rules can, for instance, (i) establish what barriers to entry are prohibited;[8] and/or (ii) what actions by members cannot be prevented.[9]

Also self-coordination arises within a set of basic rules. These rules, too, can be public rules guaranteed by the state. These rules do not concern self-coordination *itself*, but a basic framework: the real-estate market, as a self-coordinating system, is for instance generated by guaranteeing certain framework-rules, such as freedom of contract and the possibility of private ownership of land/buildings (Moroni 2018). In short, spontaneous social orders – that is, situations entailing the unintended reciprocal coordination of actions among a plurality of individuals – have to be distinguished from the system of abstract rules that contribute *indirectly* to their emergence (Moroni, 2011).

To conclude, public authorities are not absent, but, in all three cases, they have – or, in any case may have – a particular role as guarantor of the underlying framework.

The three types of self-organisation instead differ with respect to the following seven elements.

A first key difference regards their *outcomes*. Self-building regards specifically the material construction of new dwellings and buildings: its outcome is mainly physical. Self-governance mainly regards the creation of common rules and managing practices regarding collectively arranged spaces and services (without necessarily building new elements). Self-coordination regards the emergence of socio-spatial patterns in society (i.e. spontaneous orders of actions) which create a certain degree of expectations among citizens regarding the compatibility of their plans.

A second difference concerns the *degree of familiarity* among the involved actors (i.e. whether or not those involved actually know each other). In the case of self-building, the individuals involved are acquainted with each other from the outset. In the case of self-governance, the individuals involved mostly meet in the course of the process. In the case of self-coordination, many involved individuals hardly ever even meet. This is due to the sheer number of people involved in urban self-coordinating mechanisms.

A third difference concerns the *form of interaction*. In the cases of self-building and self-governance, collaboration is usually the key factor, whilst in the case of self-coordination collaboration is not necessarily required. People can interact in this case without any specific collaboration, and even through competition. As Steven Strogatz (2003: 35) observes, in many large self-coordinating systems "synchrony reflects competition, not cooperation".

A fourth difference concerns the *knowledge* that has generated the form of order in question. In the case of self-building and self-governance, the form of order (i.e. a deliberate arrangement or organisation) is generated by those who have purposely decided to create and maintain that particular kind of order. Its form will therefore largely depend on the (limited) knowledge that a specific individual or group of individuals can possess. In the case of self-coordination, the knowledge that generates and maintains the type of order (i.e. a spontaneous pattern) is that of the multitude of directly and indirectly interacting individuals who unintentionally contribute to its emergence and persistence. An order generated by self-coordination therefore embodies more knowledge than each individual or group can possess independently.

A fifth difference concerns *communication*. In the cases of self-building and self-governance, individuals can communicate directly; this is why participation in various forms is usually invoked. By contrast, in the case of self-coordination the individuals involved neither know nor meet each other personally – as already stressed – and communicate only indirectly by leaving indications to which others respond (e.g. bids on the housing market, or desire paths through spaces). In this case, individuals are links in various chains of transmission through which they receive signals enabling them to adapt their programmes to circumstances and situations that no one can completely oversee (Hayek, 1988). Incidentally, this is one of the reasons why "participation" cannot be a key strategy in the case of large self-coordinating socio-spatial systems (Pennington, 2004).

A sixth difference concerns the issue of *responsibility*. Self-building and self-governance are based upon intentional actions – single individual motivations and groups of individuals with common motivations – oriented towards a pre-determined goal. Self-building and self-governance are possible precisely because certain individuals consciously and expressly adopt certain specific ends which guide their common actions. The final arrangements are therefore present and prefigured *a priori* in the minds of the individuals involved. This cannot be said of self-coordination. In self-coordination, the individual actions constituting the system are purposeful and intentional, while the emerging patterns are not. The process of creating them is beyond individuals' control. Put differently, the general self-coordinating patterns that emerge are not part of the specific aims of the individuals who contribute to their emergence: nobody acts with the objective of establishing certain specific overall patterns of actions. In this sense, self-coordination itself does not exist *ex ante*, in all of its details, in the minds of the individuals involved, but emerges *ex post*. All this has major consequences for the issue of "responsibility" (interpreted in a descriptive and not in a normative sense). In the cases of self-building and self-governance it is possible to recognise specific

Table 3.1 Similarities and differences among self-building, self-governance and self-coordination

	Self-building	*Self-governance*	*Self-coordination*
Commonalities	Introduce a certain degree of structuration Not directed from the outside Relative independence from government		
Differences			
Outcomes	New dwellings and buildings	Common rules and service management	Expectations about compatible actions
Reciprocal knowledge among the actors involved	Present from the outset	Mainly on-going	Absent and largely impossible
Mode of interaction	Collaboration required	Collaboration required	Collaboration not necessarily required
Knowledge base	Specific knowledge of an individual or group	Specific knowledge of an individual or group	Dispersed social knowledge
Form of communication	Direct (e.g., meetings)	Direct (e.g., assemblies)	Indirect (e.g., signalling)
Responsibility	Direct, shared and intentional	Direct, shared and intentional	Indirect
Level	Plot level	Pre-targeted groups or networks	Unconstrained

groups of individuals who are *directly* responsible for the main outcomes of their projects (e.g. new houses or new community arrangements). By contrast, in the case of self-coordination, such direct responsibility is inherently absent. Intentionality is distributed among all the various individuals acting: they interfere with the process of pattern formation without being able fully to understand the effects of their involvement. Responsibility is only *indirect*.

A seventh key difference regards the *levels* (i.e. scale) at which the self-organising phenomena appear and are at work. Self-building manifests itself mainly at plot level. Processes of self-governance are oriented to pre-targeted groups within the city, ranging from street communities to city-wide collectives. In contrast, self-coordination is not constrained to any particular level of urban or supra-urban development: because it is not connected with any specific intentionality or project (as in the case of self-building and self-governance), self-coordination is not limited by the real imaginative or design capacity of a particular individual or group. Instead, self-coordination gives rise to certain inter-subjective meta-conditions (which in turn influence the actions of different individuals and organisations) *at various levels.*

3.2 Why self-organisation as self-coordination constitutes the main challenge

All the three forms of self-organisation considered here pose some kind of challenge for public planning; that is, they invite reconsideration and revision of certain consolidated views and tools.

The first case of self-organisation considered, namely *self-building*, is a challenge because it constitutes a very special channel of access to housing. Households are not mere passive consumers in this case. Rather, they are actively involved in the actual production of their homes. Generally considered as a significant practice only in certain countries of the global South (i.e. a recourse for poor areas only), actually self-building is an increasingly significant method for developed countries as well.

The second case of self-organisation considered, namely *self-governance*, represents a challenge because it constitutes an intermediate level of governance (linked to the introduction of rules and management of services) lying between public authorities and individuals or isolated families. This level of governance which is gaining traction in many countries was not always recognised as crucial in the twentieth century (sometimes, it was also explicitly hampered)[10]

The third case of self-organisation, that is, *self-coordination*, is a challenge because its (spontaneous) form of coordination does not coincide with forms of top-down coordination established by public authorities. Furthermore, its spontaneous nature prevents planners from fully understanding and anticipating the potential consequences.

In all three cases, and if we accept that something positive can be found in them, public actors can mainly act as guarantors and enablers (ensuring that they happen without any harmful repercussions). In this book we focus especially on the role that the public actor could play particularly in the third case, because we believe that it is the one most challenging for planning.[11] In this regard, note that the question of *complexity* – so widely debated today in urban studies and planning theory – almost solely concerns our third case. It is indeed self-coordination that constitutes the distinctive and central component of complex (urban) systems.

Let us consider more specifically why self-coordination is, in our view, the main challenge. The point here is that orthodox planning theory (e.g. Mumford, 1938; Abercrombie, 1943) and, very often, later planning theory (e.g. Rydin, 1993: 367), have mainly considered two alternatives to be possible: (i) *top-down coordination* (i.e. public planning) or (ii) *chaos* (i.e. anarchy and disorder).

The idea that coordination has to be imposed on otherwise uncoordinated socio-spatial systems is at the core of the very idea of planning. As Stephen Marshall (2009: 139) observes: "City planning is effectively premised on the idea of the unplanned city as disordered and dysfunctional". While this traditional attitude is partially attenuated in contemporary planning practices, discussion on how planning strategies and policies can enable, constrain, or trigger urban self-coordination is still limited (Rauws and de Roo, 2016). Therefore, the remainder of this book investigates more directly and deeply the implications of self-coordination for urban planning. Part of what follows in further chapters also applies to the other two self-organising phenomena discussed earlier. But we shall focus above all on the latter, since as already noted, it is the most challenging one as regards planning practices.[12]

The fundamental point is that self-coordination is crucial, not for putting everything in the right place, but for generating new options and possibilities which would otherwise not have actually existed (Hayek, 1988). In these cases: "We are able to bring about an ordering of the unknown only by causing it to order itself" (Hayek, 1988: 83).

4 Conclusion

This chapter has attempted, first of all, to clarify how different self-organisation processes take effect in urban environments. It has argued that: (i) self-organisation as self-building is in essence about the *enterprising autonomy* of individuals in obtaining new dwellings; (ii) self-organisation as self-governance is about the *decision-making independence* of a group of individuals to decide on their own private rules and services without the direct support of external governmental organisations; (iii) self-organisation as self-coordination is about *spontaneous alignment*; that is, the process whereby synchronisation occurs in society without being deliberately created by anybody. These self-organising phenomena share certain features. But they also have, as we evidenced, fundamental differences.

Secondly, the chapter has stressed that especially self-coordination, *as a core mechanism of complex urban systems*, poses a major challenge to urban planners and their established repertoire of tools. In what follows, whenever we mention self-organisation we will mean self-organisation as self-coordination.

Notes

1 As evidenced by the extensive critical overview by de Bruijn and Gerrits (2018).
2 See also Rauws (2016).
3 For other attempts to unpack different manifestations of urban self-organization (albeit in this case two which lead in quite different directions), see Eizenberg (2018) and Pizzo (2018).
4 For example, *self-building* as a practice of self-organisation is discussed by De Carli (2016). Self-organisation as *self-governance*, self-management, is considered, for instance, by Morales (2010), Zhou (2014); Finka and Kluvánková (2015), Edelenbos et al. (2018), Yap (2019), Hernandez et al. (2023). Urban self-organisation, understood in the strict sense of *self-coordination*, is discussed by Marchand (1984), Haken and Portugali (1995), Portugali (1999), Partanen (2015, 2020), Nunbogu and Korah (2017), Lai (2020).
5 For further reflections on self-building, see Bossuyt et al. (2018), Bossuyt (2021).
6 On energy communities (an issue that is attracting attention in both the public debate and the academic literature), see e.g. Moroni et al. (2016; 2018; 2019), Moroni and Tricarico (2018).
7 For the first case, see e.g. Andersson (2012) and Holcombe (2011); for the second, Marchand (1984), White and Engelen (1993), Schweitzer and Steinbrink (1998), Fujita et al. (1999), Haase et al. (2012); for the third, Kerner (1998), Helbing et al. (2001 and 2005), Yerra and Levinson (2005); Moussaïd et al. (2009), Helbing (2012), Miguel (2013), Hoogendoorn et al. (2014 and 2015), Goldsztein (2020), Xie et al. (2022).
8 In the United States, for example, the *Fair Housing Amendments Act* of 1988 expressly outlaws discrimination, based on skin colour, race, ethnic origin, gender, in a person's right of access to property or the use of private common services.

9 For instance, in 2011 Texas enacted the *House Bill 362*, which forbids homeowner associations from prohibiting solar-energy devices.

10 See e.g. Beito et al. (2002), Body-Gendrot et al. (2008), Brunetta and Moroni (2012), Andersson and Moroni (2014). In Italy, for instance, certain laws hampered traditional forms of collective private ownership of natural resources: in particular, law no. 1766 of 1927 introduced rigid categories that prevented a great variety of existing and possible arrangements (Lottieri, 2010).

11 Compare with Boonstra and Boelens (2011), Rauws et al. (2016), Cozzolino et al. (2017).

12 For discussion of how the role of public regulations and interventions could change in other cases of self-organization, see for example Moroni (2014).

References

Abercrombie, P. (1943). *Town and Country Planning*. London: Oxford University Press.

Andersson, D.E. (ed.) (2012). *The Spatial Market Process*. Bingley: Emerald.

Andersson, D.E., Moroni, S. (eds) (2014). *Cities and Private Planning. Property Rights, Entrepreneurship and Transaction Costs*. Cheltenham: Edward Elgar.

Beito D.T., Gordon P., Tabarrok, A. (eds) (2002). *The Voluntary City*. Ann Arbor, MI: The University of Michigan Press.

Body-Gendrot, S., Carré, J., Garbaye, R. (eds) (2008). *A City of One's Own*. Aldershot: Ashgate.

Boonstra, B., Boelens, L. (2011). Self-organization in urban development: towards a new perspective on spatial planning. *Urban Research & Practice*, 4 (2): 99–122.

Boonstra, B., Rauws, W. (2021). Ontological diversity in urban self-organization: Complexity, critical realism and post-structuralism. *Planning Theory*, 20 (4): 303–324.

Bossuyt, D.M. (2021). The value of self-build: Understanding the aspirations and strategies of owner-builders in the Homeruskwartier, Almere. *Housing Studies*, 36 (5): 696–713.

Bossuyt, D., Salet, W., Majoor, S. (2018). Commissioning as cornerstone of self-build housing. Assessing the constraints and opportunities of self-build in The Netherlands. *Land Use Policy*, 77: 524–533.

Brunetta, G., Moroni, S. (2012). *Contractual Communities in the Self-Organising City*. Berlin: Springer.

Clapham, D., Kintrea, K., McAdam, G. (1993). Individual self-provision and the Scottish housing system. *Urban Studies*, 30 (8): 1355–1369.

Cozzolino, S., Buitelaar, E., Moroni, S., Sorel, N. (2017). Experimenting in urban self-organization. Framework-rules and emerging orders in Oosterwold (Almere, The Netherlands). *Cosmos+Taxis*, 4 (2): 49–59.

de Bruijn, E., Gerrits, L. (2018). Epistemic communities in urban self-organization: A systematic review and assessment. *Journal of Planning Literature*, 33 (3): 310–328.

De Carli, B. (2016). Micro-resilience and justice: Co-producing narratives of change. *Building Research & Information*, 44 (7): 775–788.

Duncan, S.S., Rowe, A. (1993). Self-provided housing. *Urban Studies*, 30 (8): 1331–1354.

Edelenbos, J., van Meerkerk, I., Schenk, T. (2018). The evolution of community self-organization in interaction with government institutions. *The American Review of Public Administration*, 48 (1): 52–66.

Eizenberg, E. (2018). Patterns of self-organization in the context of urban planning. *Planning Theory*, 18 (1): 40–57.

Finka, M., Kluvánková, T. (2015). Managing complexity of urban systems: A polycentric approach. *Land Use Policy*, 42: 602–608.

Fujita, M., Krugman, P., Mori, T. (1999). On the evolution of hierarchical urban systems. *European Economic Review*, 43 (2): 209–251.

Goldsztein, G.H. (2020). Self-organization when pedestrians move in opposite directions. multi-lane circular track model. *Applied Sciences*, 10 (2): 1–13.

Haase, D., Haase, A., Kabisch, N., Kabisch, S., Rink, D. (2012). Actors and factors in land-use simulation. *Environmental Modelling & Software*, 35: 92–103.

Haken, H., Portugali, J. (1995). A synergetic approach to the self-organization of cities and settlements. *Environment and Planning B*, 22 (1): 35–46.

Hayek, F.A. (1988). *The Fatal Conceit*. London: Routledge.

Helbing, D., Molnár, P., Farkas, I.J., Bolay, K. (2001). Self-organizing pedestrian movement. *Environment and Planning B*, 28 (3): 361–383.

Helbing, D., Buzna, L., Johansson, A., Werner, T. (2005). Self-organized pedestrian crowd dynamics: Experiments, simulations, and design solutions. *Transportation Science*, 39 (1): 1–24.

Helbing, D. (2012). Self-organization in pedestrian crowds. In D. Helbing (ed.), *Social Self-Organization. Understanding Complex Systems*. Berlin: Springer, 71–99.

Hernandez, B., Manuel-Navarrete, D., Lerner, A.M., Siqueiros, J.M. (2023). Making informal water distribution work: collective agency and self-organization in informal areas of Xochimilco, Mexico City. *International Journal of the Commons*, 17 (1): 54–68.

Holcombe, R.G. (2011). Cultivating creativity: market creation of agglomeration economies. In D.E. Andersson, E. Andersson, C. Mellander (eds), *Handbook of Creative Cities*. Cheltenham: Edward Elgar, 387–404.

Hoogendoorn, S.P., van Wageningen-Kessels, F.L., Daamen, W., Duives, D.C. (2014). Continuum modelling of pedestrian flows: From microscopic principles to self-organised macroscopic phenomena. *Physica A: Statistical Mechanics and its Applications*, 416: 684–694.

Hoogendoorn, S.P., van Wageningen-Kessels, F., Daamen, W., Duives, D.C., Sarvi, M. (2015). Continuum theory for pedestrian traffic flow: Local route choice modelling and its implications. *Transportation Research Procedia*, 7: 381–397.

Kerner, B.S. (1998). Experimental features of self-organization in traffic flow. *Physical Review Letters*, 81 (17): 3797–3800.

Lai, S.K. (2020). Evidence of urban spatial self-organization. *Journal of Urban Management*, 9 (4): 1–4.

Lottieri, C. (2010). Usi civici e città volontaria. In C. Lottieri (ed.), *Dalle vicinie al federalismo*. Pordenone: Associazione Carlo Cattaneo, 47–93.

Marchand, B. (1984). Urban growth models revisited: Cities as self-organizing systems. *Environment and Planning A*, 16 (7): 949–964.

Marshall, S. (2009). *Cities, Design and Evolution*. London: Routledge.

Miguel, A.F. (2013). The emergence of design in pedestrian dynamics: Locomotion, self-organization, walking paths and constructal law. *Physics of Life Reviews*, 10 (2): 168–190.

Morales, A. (2010). Planning and the self-organization of marketplaces. *Journal of Planning Education and Research*, 30 (2): 182–197.

Moroni, S. (2011). The role of deliberate intervention on organizations and institutions. *Planning Theory*, 10 (2): 190–197.

Moroni, S. (2014). Towards a general theory of contractual communities. In D.E. Andersson, S. Moroni (eds), *Cities and Private Planning*. Cheltenham: Edward Elgar, 38–65.

Moroni, S. (2018). Property as a human right and property as a special title. Rediscussing private ownership of land. *Land Use Policy*, 70, 273–280.

Moroni, S., Antoniucci, V., Bisello, A. (2016). Energy sprawl, land taking and distributed generation: towards a multi-layered density. *Energy Policy*, 98: 266–273.

Moroni, S., Alberti, V., Antoniucci, V., Bisello, A. (2018). Energy communities in a distributed-energy scenario: Four different kinds of community arrangements. In A. Bisello, D. Vettorato, P. Laconte, S. Costa (eds), *Smart and Sustainable Planning for Cities and Regions*. Berlin: Springer, 429–437.

Moroni, S., Antoniucci, V., Bisello, A. (2019). Local energy communities and distributed generation. *Sustainability*, 11 (12): 1–16.

Moroni, S., Tricarico, L. (2018). Distributed energy production in a polycentric scenario: policy reforms and community management. *Journal of Environmental Planning and Management*, 61 (11): 1973–1993.

Moussaïd, M., Helbing, D., Garnier, S., Johansson, A., Combe, M., Theraulaz, G. (2009). Experimental study of the behavioural mechanisms underlying self-organization in human crowds. *Proceedings of the Royal Society B: Biological Sciences*, 276 (1668): 2755–2762.

Mumford, L. (1938). *The Culture of Cities*. San Diego, CA: Harcourt Brace.

Nunbogu, A.M., Korah, P.I. (2017). Self-organisation in urban spatial planning: Evidence from the Greater Accra Metropolitan Area, Ghana. *Urban Research & Practice*, 10 (4): 423–441.

Partanen, J. (2015). Indicators for self-organization potential in urban context. *Environment and Planning B*, 42 (5): 951–971.

Partanen, J. (2020). Guiding urban self-organization: Combining rule-based and case-based planning. *Environment and Planning B*, 47 (2): 304–320.

Pennington, M. (2004). Citizen participation, the knowledge problem and urban land use planning. *The Review of Austrian Economics*, 17 (2): 213–231.

Pizzo, B. (2018). The many paths of self-organization. *Tracce Urbane*, 2 (4): 49–67.

Portugali, J. (1999). *Self-Organization and the City*. Berlin: Springer.

Rauws, W. (2016). Civic initiatives in urban development: self-governance versus self-organisation in planning practice. *Town Planning Review*, 87 (3): 339–361.

Rauws, W., de Roo, G. (2016). Adaptive planning: Generating conditions for urban adaptability. *Environment and Planning B*, 43 (6): 1052–1074.

Rauws, W., de Roo, G., Zhang, S. (2016). Self-organisation and spatial planning. *Town Planning Review*, 87 (3): 241–251.

Rydin, Y. (1993). *The British Planning System*. London: Macmillan.

Schweitzer, F., Steinbrink, J. (1998). Estimation of megacity growth: simple rules versus complex phenomena. *Applied Geography*, 18 (1): 69–81.

Strogatz, S. (2003). *Sync: How Order Emerges from Chaos in the Universe, Nature, and Daily Life*. New York: Hyperion.

White, R., Engelen, G. (1993). Cellular automata and fractal urban form. *Environment and planning A*, 25(8): 1175–1199.

Xie, W., Lee, E.W.M., Lee, Y.Y. (2022). Self-organisation phenomena in pedestrian counter flows and its modelling. *Safety Science*, 155: 1–15.

Yap, C. (2019). Self-organisation in urban community gardens: Autogestion, motivations, and the role of communication. *Sustainability*, 11 (9): 1–21.

Yerra, B.M., Levinson, D.M. (2005). The emergence of hierarchy in transportation networks. *The Annals of Regional Science*, 39: 541–553.

Zhou, M. (2014). Debating the State in private housing neighborhoods: The governance of homeowners' associations in urban Shanghai. *International Journal of Urban and Regional Research*, 38 (5): 1849–1866.

4 Property

1 Introduction

Cities evolve in ways that are largely emergent and centrally controllable only to a limited extent. As Karl Kropf (2009: 106) emphasises, "cities are the result of deliberate and coordinated human effort on the one hand and exhibit characteristics of self-organisation and emergent behaviour on the other".[1] Nevertheless, it is important to stress that not all cities work in exactly the same way. In fact, the potential for the generation of emergent and self-generated patterns in cities may manifest itself to different extents. This variance also depends on the presence of *multiple* urban agents able to act directly and of their own accord. This explains why certain cities, or part(s) of them, are very dynamic and grow spontaneously over time, while others are less open to the emergence of spontaneous configurations and are, so to speak, more "designed". In short, cities are places where the trade-off between *design/control* and *spontaneity/emergence* is constantly present and spatially expressed (Ikeda, 2017).

Although it is now recognised in the planning literature that the main constituent driver of complex cities is action, to date little attention has been paid to how *property* (in its connection with action) and *property patterns* can trigger or discourage the propensity of cities to rely on the evolution of emergent configurations. This chapter focuses on this under-explored issue.

Before beginning the discussion, some fundamental specifications, concerning *action* and *property*, are necessary.

As we have seen (Chapter 2), "action" can be defined as the intentional and purposeful behaviour of urban subjects who implement specific independent plans to achieve certain desired changes. Actions always occur in situations of real time and space and are developed according to the subjective desires, means, and contextual (mainly

DOI: 10.4324/9781003454304-4

tacit) knowledge through which (urban) agents interpret existing social-spatial conditions and discover feasible opportunities. As already underscored, an action does not necessarily have to be understood as exclusively undertaken by a single, isolated person. An action can be undertaken by a single individual or by a group of individuals acting in concert. The kinds of urban action that are crucial in our perspective are the acts of moulding, transforming, and adapting the urban fabric and its uses (and obviously all the ancillary actions helpful in this regard, including obtaining loans and signing agreements and covenants). In other words, we suggest focusing on urban subjects that act in order to construct a new building, modify the internal and external appearance of a certain structure, or convert the use of an already existing space. These are the kinds of actions that continuously and incrementally shape and re-shape the built environment, giving it the capacity to persist and evolve over time through self-adapting processes of change. Moreover, these are the kinds of actions that enable urban agents to constantly improve their environments by providing concrete answers to their specific needs and desires (Brand, 1995; Habraken, 1998). If we take the role of action (*in* and *for* self-generating processes of change in cities) into serious account, *property* cannot but be a crucial factor. In fact, property in the built environment directly involves the question of who can make decisions about certain spatial changes and adaptions, and act accordingly (Kropf, 2018).

"Property" is a socially acknowledged relation between an urban agent and an urban object (such as a building) that confers upon him/her a certain *power of action* and control over that object.[2] The agent in a position to exercise such power of action and control is the *owner*. This power is indeed the essence of ownership. As Butler Shaffer (2009: 161) aptly points out, "to be an owner of anything is to be the effective decision-maker over such an item of property". Also here, some clarifications may be useful to prevent possible misunderstandings. First, it is obviously important to maintain the distinction between *private* and *public property*. In the case of private property, urban agents should be able to direct the use of a property towards their independent self-interests (within mutual constraints). In the case of public property, by contrast, the use of any property comes to be defined politically in the name of the public interest (Moroni, 2004, 2018b). In this chapter, we will focus mainly on private property.[3] As we shall see in the next section, the general category of "private property" is however insufficient in itself to represent the numerous possible facets of private property regimes,[4] and their inherent degree of complexity in decision-making processes regarding, for instance, the present or future uses of a specific building or structure (Slaev, 2020). Second, it is necessary to clarify the difference between (i) the "general right to hold private property" and (ii) "specific property titles". In the former case, such a basic right refers to the formal possibility of *any agent* to become the owner of something (e.g. a building), whereas the latter case refers to the specific entitlement of *an agent* to a specific object (e.g. building A in city B). The point is that the formal "right to hold private property" may be granted to anyone, while "specific property titles" are the result of legal/market transactions and acquisitions over time, and they pertain to individual persons (Moroni, 2018a, 2019, 2022).

In this chapter, we assume that individuals have the fundamental right to own private property, focusing instead on how property titles are spatially configured and distributed.

To conclude: property provides a crucial means by which a person is able to act within (and adapt) the built environment.[5] More importantly, the spatial distribution of property allocates "control responsibilities" within urban contexts and influences the self-adapting propensity of cities. For this reason, the overall structure of property patterns is of key importance in understanding the distribution of design responsibility among different urban agents in space (Akbar, 1988; Babie, 2013), social-economic urban processes (Ellickson, 1993; Dixon, 2009), and the way in which the built environment performs and evolves over time (Bobkova et al., 2018).

2 Focus: A matrix of property arrangements

To provide an overview of different patterns of (private) property and to understand their implications for the propensity of urban areas to generate and accommodate self-adaptive processes of change, we assume that two main factors should be considered: (i) the *scale* of an urban object (to which property titles are linked) and (ii) the *types of property* held in that object. Considering these two factors, it is possible to create a matrix that evidences various (private) property patterns. This is clearly an abstract schema but it can nevertheless provide significant insights for the discussion of self-adapting phenomena in cities.[6]

2.1 Scale of the urban object

We consider an *urban object* to be a unitarily managed area/space (e.g. one building or an ensemble of buildings and spaces) subject to the power of action and control of one specific *agent* (that agent being an individual owner, either natural or legal, or multiple co-owners acting in concert) directly responsible for its present and future uses. In this regard, we identify three main possibilities, namely, (i) *single buildings*, (ii) *sets of buildings*, and (iii) *neighbourhood units* (Figure 4.1). The building is chosen here as the smallest item for our analysis. (The approach might obviously be extended to comprise even smaller items like single dwellings). It is important to stress that neighbourhoods with a single private owner were not so uncommon in the past.[7] Interesting cases are observable also today.[8] However, this option is mainly a conceptually (and logically) crucial possibility.

i Single buildings. In this case, an agent has a certain power of action and control over only one specific building. Given their different impacts in the system, in this category it is important to distinguish between a small-scale building (as would be the case of a two-storey building in a compact and dense urban tissue) and a

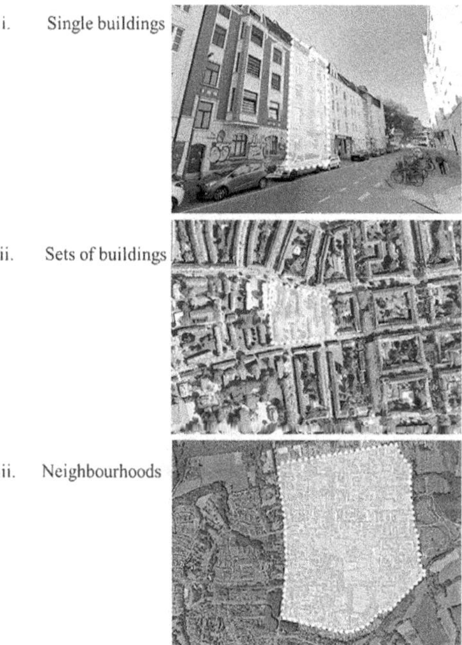

Figure 4.1 Scale of the urban object
Source: Imagery @2023 Google, Map data @2023 Google.

large-scale building (as in the case of one large hangar or an office skyscraper).

ii Sets of buildings. In this case, an urban agent has a certain power of action and control over multiple buildings clustered together. In this category it is important to distinguish between a set of prevalently small-scale buildings and a set composed of prevalently large-scale ones.

iii Neighbourhoods. In this case, an urban agent has a certain power of action and control over an extended urban area such as a neighbourhood unit. In this category, it may be again important to distinguish between a neighbourhood prevalently composed of small-scale buildings and a unit prevalently composed of large-scale ones.

2.2 *Types of properties*

A property can assume a simple configuration and be owned by a single owner, or it can be more complex, as in the case of a group of individuals sharing decision-making responsibility for commonly owned property. In this regard, we identify three possible *types* of ownership of a specific urban object: (i) *simple*, (ii) *hybrid*, and (iii) *collective* (Figure 4.2). Different property types affect the way in which urban objects are effectively managed and organised and therefore the decision-making processes concerning their present and future use. Observe that the number of individuals sharing the ownership of a certain object directly influences the degree of simplicity or complexity of decision-making processes in regard to that ownership,[9] with smaller groups being, in general, more effective.[10] Large groups often present a "tragedy of the anti-commons" problem: a situation in which, given the presence of many subjects sharing rights on a certain common property, action is largely discouraged (Heller, 1998). Many of the examples in what follows are taken from the residential sector, but the same types of property configurations also apply to commercial units, industrial plants and office districts (and to various mixes of them).

i Simple property. A simple property situation is one in which a single owner is directly responsible for the present and future uses of a specific object (be it a single building, a set of buildings or a neighbourhood unit). In this case, the decision-making process is simple because the owner can freely choose his or her actions without (direct) interference by someone else.

ii Hybrid property. This is the ownership situation typical of condominiums (Lee, 1989), co-housing units (Chiodelli and Baglione,

2014) and homeowner associations (Lai, 2016). The distinctive feature of this type of ownership is that while all individuals are usually responsible for a certain amount of private space where they can act rather independently (as in the case of a private apartment in a condominium complex), they also share responsibility for some common spaces that require acting in concert (in a condominium complex, examples of these spaces are common green areas, stairwells, building façades, walkways and rooftops). With this type of property, the decision-making process is relatively simple with regard to the management and use of private spaces, while the process is more complex in the case of common spaces where individuals must agree on the same concerted action. Common spaces of this kind present typical collective action problems. Obviously, the degree of complexity in the management of common spaces increases if the number of individuals with the right to participate in the decision-making process also increases.

iii Collective property. A collective property is one in which a group of individuals share common responsibility for the present and future uses of a whole object, as in the case of commons (van Gils et al., 2014) or residential cooperatives (Sazama, 2000). In the case of residential cooperatives, it is the co-op that usually owns the buildings, and common areas, while members each own a co-op share. In situations like cooperatives and commons, any change in the property or any part of it requires a shared "protocol" – such as a voting procedure based on unanimity or nearly-unanimity – that all members must respect. This means that in the case of collective property, an individual is not free to act of his or her own accord without "interference". He or she needs to abide by the processes of the mediation and the collective acceptance of

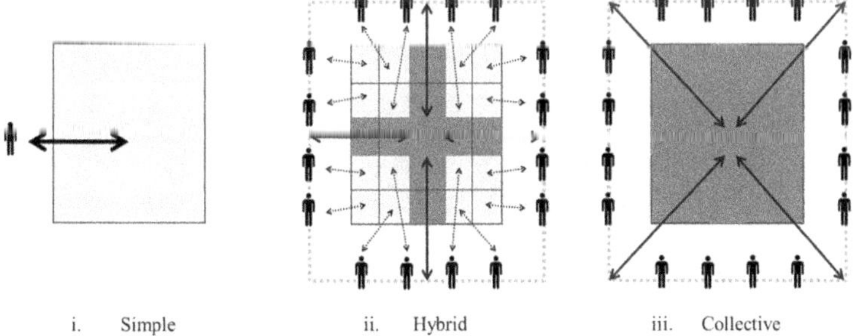

Figure 4.2 Types of properties

his or her action by the other members. Also in this case, the degree of complexity in the decision-making process increases as the number of members participating in management and decision-making increases.

2.3 A general schema

In summary, our suggestion is to distinguish different ownership patterns and the resulting differences in the distribution of design responsibility in the built environment according to two main factors: first, the *scale of urban objects*, which refers to (i) single buildings, (ii) sets of buildings, or (iii) neighbourhood; and, second, the *type of ownership*, which can be (i) simple, (ii) hybrid, or (iii) collective. In this regard, we have a nine-cell matrix that illustrates the various possibilities (Table 4.1). This matrix also represents a schema useful for understanding the propensity of an urban object or an ensemble of objects to accommodate new actions and therefore be reused and adapted over time. As already underscored, this matrix is a sort of schematic simplification. However, we think that this abstract schema can effectively address the crux of the issue.

In Cells 1, 4 and 7 we have the case of a single building, for example a three-storey building located in a city centre. Cell 1 is the situation in which the building has a single owner. Cell 4 is for example the case of a traditional condominium. Cell 7 is the case of a traditional urban residential cooperative. In Cells 2, 5 and 8 we have sets of buildings (be they all of the same type – e.g. residential – or of different types). Cell 2 is again the case of a single owner (a natural or legal person).

Table 4.1 Nine possible ownership arrangements

		Scale of the object		
		Single buildings	*Set of buildings*	*Neighbourhoods/parts of cities*
Type of property	*Simple*	Cell 1: Simple ownership of a building	Cell 2: Simple ownership of a set of buildings	Cell 3: Simple ownership of an entire neighbourhood
	Hybrid	Cell 4: Hybrid ownership of a single building	Cell 5: Hybrid ownership of a set of buildings	Cell 6: Hybrid ownership of an entire neighbourhood
	Collective	Cell 7: Collective ownership of a single building	Cell 8: Collective ownership of a set of buildings	Cell 9: Collective ownership of an entire neighbourhood

Cell 5 is for instance exemplified by super-condominiums, comprising more residential building units. Cell 8 is the situation of wide cooperative arrangements. In Cells 3, 6 and 9 we have parts of the city with many different buildings, structures and spaces. Cell 3 is the case of a single owner, as in the case of certain neighbourhood units, or even vast shopping centres or big entertainment complexes. Cell 6 is the situation of, for instance, large homeowners' associations or particular business districts. Cell 9 is the situation of very huge cooperatives or other kinds of common arrangements concerning entire sectors of a city.

3 Discussion: Property patterns and openness to emergence

The two factors combined – *scale* of urban objects and *type* of property – tell us something interesting concerning the spatial distribution of the power of action and control in the built environment.

Firstly, we may observe that (the presence of many) large-scale objects often impede fast rearrangements. By contrast, in the case of a multiplicity of smaller-scale objects, it is easier to make rearrangements. The same applies to property titles: complex property titles in which many decision makers are involved usually adapt more slowly over time, while simple property titles are, at least potentially, more flexible and responsive.

A second important implication concerns the question of the concentration – and dispersion – of the power of action and design responsibility in space. Whilst a large-scale property usually implies that broad spatial control is concentrated in the hands of a single agent (or multiple agents acting in concert), the presence of many smaller-scale properties implies the opposite: that is, the distribution of spatial control is in the hands of multiple and independent urban agents (Louw, 2008; Gallagher et al., 2019).

From an analysis of the *scale* and *type* of property of all "objects" included in a certain area, it is therefore possible to obtain an initial general idea of the overall propensity of that area to rely on emergent processes of change. A densely populated urban area consisting mainly of single buildings with simple ownership is, for instance, an area where the power of action and control is distributed among many independent urban agents. The area is therefore potentially more inclined to rely on emergent processes of change. Conversely, an area consisting mainly of large-scale urban objects with hybrid or collective ownership is an area where the power of action and control is more concentrated. Therefore, this area is potentially less inclined to spontaneous evolution.

Based on this idea, it is likely that within a specific area, the larger the number of urban agents in a position to act upon and adapt the built environment directly and without intermediation, the greater the overall propensity of that area to rely on emergent processes of change.

A tentative empirical analysis to test this hypothesis yielded promising results. We conducted an exercise in Dortmund (Germany). First, we mapped building ownership types. Second, we selected those areas above a minimum threshold of building density and calculated the percentage of buildings with simple ownership types per unit of analysis. In this way, we were able to identify and distinguish those areas potentially more inclined to undergo emergent processes of change from areas potentially less inclined to do so (because they were prevalently characterised by hybrid or collective types of ownership in unitarily managed groups of buildings). In the two areas in Dortmund that appeared to be those with potentially higher emergent propensities the power of action and design responsibility are distributed among multiple independent owners.[11]

4 Conclusion

The spatial dimension and organisation of property is often underestimated. However, if we consider the importance of action *in* and *for* urban adaptation, property cannot but be an aspect indispensable for understanding the propensity of cities to evolve (more or less) spontaneously over time. A self-organising city, in fact, is one in which a certain power of action on urban objects is dispersed among many urban agents and not just a few. All of this guarantees space for experimentation, trial-and-error processes of change and, therefore, innovations and adaptations unachievable in a situation of extended centralised (private or public) control.

The view presented in this chapter is primarily explanatory and descriptive (as we will see in the Annex, it can be utilised in the development of novel forms of urban analysis grounded in property typology and patterns). Clearly, the chapter also indirectly provides additional insights for a strategic and normative approach; however, to avoid misunderstandings, it is important to underscore that the point is not that "small is (always) better" *per se*: rather, it is that *variety* and *polycentrism* (of property assets) are crucial (as we will see in Chapter 7).

Notes

1 On this point, see also Kostof (1991).
2 This power (of action and control) is obviously not "absolute" because it is usually exercised within a common, reciprocal rule-framework. On this issue, see e.g. Akbar (1988).
3 The role that *publicly* owned spaces and structures can have *in* and *for* complex cities will be discussed in Chapter 7.
4 See on this Ellickson (1993); Chiodelli and Moroni (2014); Nachmany and Hananel (2019).
5 The focus of this chapter is therefore mainly on owners; obviously, the analysis could be extended and enriched to consider tenants as well.
6 Similar observations on how the scale of urban objects and their property may influence the self-coordinating capacity of urban systems are also put forward by Brand (1995), Habraken (2008), Alterman (2010), Love and Crawford (2011), Renae Johnston and Reid (2013), Hausleitner and Nycolaas (2014), Webb and Webber (2017), and McGreevy (2017). Without doubt, however, the first to raise this question was Jacobs (1961).
7 For example, during the 18th and 19th centuries, it was common for a landowner in London to transform and urbanise certain large areas and then lease the buildings to a variety of tenants. The (single) owner continued to attend to the management and administration of the entire complex (Summerson, 1962; Olsen, 1964; Rasmussen, 1967; Booth, 2003).
8 There are today many cases of large settlements owned and managed by, for instance, housing associations and cooperatives. For example, in Dortmund (Germany), the SPARBAU housing cooperative owns (and rents) about 12,000 apartments, many of them clustered in Scharnhorst-Ost. Other examples of neighbourhood-like units (with a single owner) are private campuses, large commercial districts, big entertainment complexes (like *Walt Disney World* – Florida), and mega hotels (like the *MGM Grand* or the *Venetian* in Las Vegas – Nevada) (Moroni, 2014; Brunetta and Moroni, 2012).
9 As Hansmann (1991: 34) write: "A potentially significant source of costs in residential cooperatives and condominiums, though one that is not often discussed, lies in the collective decision-making mechanisms that these forms require". He notes: If the interests of all members of the condominium or cooperative were identical, "the decisions they made collectively would presumably be efficient. In fact, however, their interests often diverge substantially"; on the one hand, members vary in their desires: "some will be satisfied with wood-grained vinyl for the elevator walls, while others will strongly prefer spending what is necessary to have real wood; some will want better laundry facilities in the basement, while those who take their laundry out or have their own machines will not"; on the other hand, preferences will diverge "because the members' apartments differ in structure or location: those on the ground floor may be less eager than those on the top floor to refurbish the elevators" (Hansmann, 1991: 34). Moreover, "there may be substantial transaction costs associated with the process of making collective decisions in a cooperative or condominium, such as the time that the occupants vote to meetings and other governance activities"; by contrast, "a single individual acting as landlord

can presumably collect information and make decisions with less expenditure of effort" (Hansmann, 1991: 34).

10 On this, see e.g. Olson (1965), Orban (2006), Yau (2014).

11 The two areas that appeared to be those with potentially higher emergent propensities were Kreuzviertel and Nordstadt. These two neighbourhoods have totally different reputations in the city of Dortmund. Kreuzviertel is considered to be an exclusive and attractive neighbourhood. Conversely, Nordstadt is an area that is stigmatised for certain social issues and is one of the cheapest areas of Dortmund. Notwithstanding their different reputations, these two neighbourhoods present certain similar features. One important shared feature is the number and concentration of different functions and uses that turn these areas into two highly vibrant zones in Dortmund. In the Annex, we will take a closer look at this case.

References

Akbar, J. (1988). *Crisis in the Built Environment.* Singapore: Concept Media Pte Ltd.

Alterman, R. (2010). The maintenance of residential towers in condominium tenure: A comparative analysis of two extremes – Israel and Florida. In S. Blandy, A. Dupuis, J.E. Dixon (eds), *Multi-Owned Housing.* Farnham: Ashgate, 126–142.

Babie, P. (2013). The spatial: A forgotten dimension of property. *San Diego Law Review*, 50: 323–382.

Bobkova, E., Marcus, L., Berghauser Pont, M. (2018). Plot systems and property rights: morphological, juridical and economic aspects. In D. Urios, J. Colomer, A. Portalés (eds), *24th ISUF International Conference. Book of Papers.* Valencia: Editorial Universitat Politècnica de València, 177–185.

Booth, P. (2003). *Planning by Consent.* London: Routledge.

Brand, S. (1995). *How Buildings Learn.* London: Penguin.

Brunetta, G., Moroni, S. (2012). *Contractual Communities in the Self-Organising City.* Berlin: Springer.

Chiodelli, F., Baglione, V. (2014). Living together privately: For a cautious reading of cohousing. *Urban Research & Practice*, 7 (1): 20–34.

Chiodelli, F., Moroni, S. (2014). Typology of spaces and topology of toleration: City, pluralism, ownership. *Journal of Urban Affairs*, 36 (2): 167–181.

Dixon, T. (2009). Urban land and property ownership patterns in the UK: Trends and forces for change. *Land Use Policy*, 26: 43–53.

Ellickson, R.C. (1993). Property in land. *Yale Law Journal*, 102: 1315–1400.

Gallagher, R., Liu, Y., Sigler, T. (2019). Parcel amalgamation as a mechanism for achieving urban consolidation through densification: The fixity of property boundaries over time. *Land Use Policy*, 89: 1–11.

Habraken, N.J. (1998). *The Structure of the Ordinary: Form and Control in the Built Environment.* Cambridge, MA: The MIT Press.

Habraken, N.J. (2008). Design for flexibility. *Building Research & Information*, 36 (3): 290–296.

Hansmann, H. (1991). Condominium and cooperative housing: Transactional efficiency, tax subsidies, and tenure choice. *The Journal of Legal Studies*, 20 (1): 25–71.

Hausleitner, B., Nycolaas, F. (2014). Physical and administrative units in the urban block in Amsterdam. In R. Cavallo, S. Komossa, N. Marzot (eds), *New Urban Configurations.* Amsterdam: IOS, 839–847.

Heller, M.A. (1998). The tragedy of the anticommons: Property in the transition from Marx to markets. *Harvard Law Review*, 111 (3): 621–688.

Ikeda, S. (2017). The city cannot be a work of art. *Cosmos and Taxis*, 4 (2/3): 79–86.

Jacobs, J. (1961). *The Death and Life of Great American Cities.* New York: Random House.

Kostof, S. (1991). *The City Shaped: Urban Patterns and Meanings through History.* London: Thames & Hudson.

Kropf, K. (2009). Aspects of urban form. *Urban Morphology*, 13 (2): 105–120.

Kropf, K. (2018). Plots, property and behaviour. *Urban Morphology*, 22 (1): 5–14.

Lai, L.W. (2016). Stone walls do not a prison make, nor iron bars a cage: The institutional and communitarian possibilities of gated communities. *Land Use Policy*, 54: 378–385.

Lee, S.L. (1989). Residential land use policy and condominium housing development. *Land Use Policy*, 6 (2): 121–131.

Louw, E. (2008). Land assembly for urban transformation. The case of 's-Hertogenbosch in The Netherlands. *Land Use Policy*, 25 (1): 69–80.

Love, T., Crawford, C. (2011). Plot logic: Character-building through creative parcelisation. In S. Tiesdel, D. Adams (eds), *Urban Design in the Real Estate Development Process.* Oxford: Wiley-Blackwell, 92–113.

McGreevy, M.P. (2017). Complexity as the telos of postmodern planning and design: Designing better cities from the bottom-up. *Planning Theory*, 17 (3): 355–374.

Moroni, S. (2004). Towards a reconstruction of the public interest criterion. *Planning Theory*, 3 (2): 151–171.

Moroni, S. (2014). Towards a general theory of contractual communities. In D.E. Andersson, S. Moroni (eds), *Cities and Private Planning.* Cheltenham: Edward Elgar, 38–65.

Moroni, S. (2018a). Property as a human right and property as a special title. Rediscussing private ownership of land. *Land Use Policy*, 70, 273–280.

Moroni, S. (2018b). Public interest. In M. Gunder, A. Madanipour, V. Watson (eds), *The Routledge Handbook of Planning Theory.* London: Routledge, 69–80.

Moroni, S. (2019). Constitutional and post-constitutional problems: Reconsidering the issues of public interest, agonistic pluralism and private property in planning. *Planning Theory*, 18 (1): 5–23.

Moroni S (2022). Rediscussing Robert Nozick's "Anarchy, State and Utopia", 1974: Property Titles to Land and Issues of Distributive Justice. In C. Perrone (ed.), *Critical Planning and Design.* Berlin: Springer, 157–168.

Nachmany, H., Hananel, R. (2019). A tale of two neighborhoods: Toward a new typology of land rights. *Land Use Policy*, 80: 233–245.

Olsen, D.J. (1964). *Town Planning in London*. New Haven: Yale University Press.

Olson, M. (1965). *Logic of Collective Action*. Cambridge, MA: Harvard University Press.

Orban, A. (2006). *Community Action for Collective Goods*. Budapest: Akademaiai Kiado.

Rasmussen, S.E. (1967). *London: The Unique City*. Cambridge, MA: The MIT Press.

Renae Johnston, N., Reid, S. (2013). Multi-owned developments: A life cycle review of a developing research area. *Property Management*, 31 (5): 366–388.

Sazama, G.W. (2000). Lessons from the history of affordable housing cooperatives in the United States. *American Journal of Economics and Sociology*, 59: 573–608.

Shaffer, B.D. (2009). *Boundaries of Order*. Auburn, AL: Ludwig von Mises Institute.

Slaev, A.D. (2020). Complex private-common property rights in institutional and planning theories. *Planning Theory*, 19 (2): 193–213.

Summerson, J. (1962). *Georgian London*. London: Barrie and Jenkins.

van Gils, H., Siegl, G., Bennett, R.M. (2014). The living commons of West Tyrol, Austria: Lessons for land policy and land administration. *Land Use Policy*, 38: 16–25.

Webb, B., Webber, S. (2017). The implications of condominium neighbourhoods for long-term urban revitalisation. *Cities*, 61: 48–57.

Yau, Y. (2014). Perceived efficacies and collectivism in multi-owned housing management. *Habitat International*, 43: 133–141.

5 Adaptability

1 Introduction

This chapter explores the features of those neighbourhoods, mainly constructed in the twentieth century, that we suggest can be called *anti-adaptive-neighbourhoods* (henceforth AANs). The existence and formation of AANs is a relatively recent phenomenon in urban history. A primary feature of areas of this kind is that, regardless of continuously changing socio-economic circumstances, their initial design structure is not prone to self-adaptive processes of change. In other words, AANs are resistant to change; this makes them less conducive to functional experimentation for new purposes and conditions, and threatens their long-term survival (Tunstall, 2016).

In contemporary cities, AANs represent a normal way of life for many people, and they are easy to find everywhere around the globe (for some examples, see Figures 5.1, 5.2 and 5.3). Sometimes these areas were first built and managed by public agencies and then partially privatised (Rowlands et al., 2009). In other cases, AANs were directly constructed by private developers, as in the case of new, large condominium ensembles (Blandy et al., 2010). Nowadays, it is still possible to observe the construction of new AANs in countries where the demographic trends are relatively stable (if not sometimes shrinking) and in countries now experiencing economic booms and high growth rates.[1]

Since Jane Jacobs' groundbreaking work (1961), reflections on the problems deriving from certain large residential areas (often inspired by the modern idea of *neighbourhood units*: Perry, 1929) have developed.[2] One criticism, in particular, concerns the inability of these areas to self-regenerate over time.

Although the literature has already investigated this issue in general terms, the discussion here redirects the attention to certain

DOI: 10.4324/9781003454304-5

Figure 5.1 La Clementina, Bergamo (Italy)
Source: Imagery @2023 Google, Map data @2023 Google.

Figure 5.2 Poleg, Netanya (Israel)
Source: Imagery @2023 Google, Map data @2023 Google.

Figure 5.3 Scharnhorst-Ost, Dortmund (Germany)
Source: Imagery @2023 Google, Map data @2023 Google.

underestimated specific aspects (crucial for understanding the adaptive or anti-adaptive capacities of neighbourhoods) by examining them through the lenses of *action* and *complexity.*

In particular, this chapter presents a theoretical framework focused on the formation of AANs, their salient features, and the primary responsibilities of planners for their generation and perpetuation.

2 Focus: The rise and problems of AANs

2.1 From adaptive to anti-adaptive

On the neighbourhood scale, adaptability is commonly considered an essential factor for two main reasons: endurance and innovation.

Firstly, an adaptive built environment is more resistant in the long run. As John Habraken (1998: 7) aptly underscores, "continuous renewal and replacements preserve it, giving it the ability to persist". The possibility to adjust the physical and functional characteristics of an urban area according to ever-evolving needs represents the key to its survival.

Secondly, adaptability welcomes innovation – especially micro-innovation – by making more efficient use of so-called *dispersed* or *local* knowledge (Chapter 2). In this way, owners, dwellers, and users can renovate, over time, the urban fabric by allowing the socio-spatial system to adjust incrementally and dynamically.[3] Besides being responsive to changes, adaptive urban areas may also favour the production and evolution of unique local urban features and identities.

In short, an adaptive urban area guarantees a significant *action space* and the possibility for complexity to emerge. On the contrary, AANs offer almost no opportunity for their inhabitants to express themselves spatially by, for example, customising or re-functioning their neighbourhood's buildings and open spaces. This condition has noticeable spatial effects: the flatness, inexpressiveness, and lack of diversity of many urban contexts where individuals can hardly undertake new actions other than ones inside their own apartments.

Only a few scholars have investigated the question of urban adaptability from a historical perspective. Among them, there are Jane Jacobs (1961), Christopher Alexander (1979), Jamel Akbar (1988), John Habraken (1998), Marco Romano (2010), and Besim Hakim (2014). Despite their diverse cultural backgrounds and approaches, these authors agree that traditional cities – for instance, the cities built before the 1900s in Europe and more in general in the Mediterranean area – are praiseworthy not only for their aesthetic character but, more importantly, for their ability to adapt and stimulate urban life. They agree that many traditional cities closely resembled a complex and adaptive living system.

In contrasting the functioning of certain traditional cities with the inflexible nature of many modern neighbourhoods, these and other authors[4] emphasise the problems that arise from constructing large urban areas all at once from scratch, and they shed light on the potential of instead embracing open-ended, incremental development processes.

Clearly, in comparing modern and traditional built environments, adaptability cannot be reduced to a black-and-white issue. In recent decades, the construction of AANs has shown both positive and negative aspects. On the one hand, AANs have in some cases been successful in responding, in the short term, to significant housing pressures (e.g. during great migrations or economic booms), in coping with various types of housing emergency, in generating opportunities for individuals and families to find affordable dwellings. On the other hand, as mentioned, these neighbourhoods have also generated undesirable effects. Particularly, AANs have exhibited scant openness to adaptation and an overall resistance to forms of incremental development and adjustment. Built rapidly, as time has passed AANs have remained largely unchanged, if not sometimes incurring processes of decline.[5]

Many of the scholars who compare the traditional and the modern city focus on the different architectural appearances and forms of their built environments. In adopting a complexity perspective, the focus is not only on this aspect (i.e. the shape and form of the built environment) but also, and primarily, on the conditions that furnish the action space necessary for long-term adaptability. According to Jamel Akbar (1988: 7), a fundamental question is the following: “Why, rather than investigating the societal process that produced the traditional environment, are we only analysing the end-product?”.

In brief, the focus should be on the *conditions of actions*: the institutional and design framework from which adaptive urban areas can eventually emerge. Therefore, comparing the principles behind the development of the traditional city with AANs does not mean assuming a nostalgic view or advocating a return to the past. Instead, it means investigating the conditions that allowed the emergence of complex-adaptive (i.e. incremental, open-ended, and largely spontaneous) development processes. The main idea is that something innovative can be learned by rediscovering past experiences.

2.2 A brief historical overview

2.2.1 The adaptive genesis of the traditional city

Henri Pirenne (1927) maintains that the roots of traditional European cities were grounded at the beginning of the eleventh century.

From that period onwards, the widespread possibility of citizens to express themselves publicly in the urban fabric by constructing their buildings became the driving force behind the formation and expansion of many traditional cities. According to Marco Romano (2010: 25–26; our translation), the emerging spatial result of the shape and appearance of the traditional city was the fruit of the "deliberate aesthetic will of their citizens, expressed in their dwellings and their facades".

Contrary to what many may think, the incremental process through which most traditional cities evolved did not occur in a regulatory vacuum. Their evolution was neither fully unplanned nor unregulated. It was governed by general *codes* aimed at "ensuring that minimum damage occurred to pre-existing structures and their owners, stipulating fairness in the distribution of rights and responsibilities among various parties, particularly those who were proximate to each other" (Hakim, 2014: 97). Following principles of this kind, changes in the built environment were accepted when new actions did not compromise the rights of others' households.

Households were generally free to do what they wanted within the constraints and conditions deriving from neighbouring properties and rights. Beyond the regulatory function of codes, municipalities also assumed responsibility for developing essential public works and spaces, such as major streets and squares, which played a key role in the expansion of cities. Moreover, the traditional practice of *covenants* (i.e. rules and restrictions on land and building use and transformation mutually accepted through private agreements) added significant space also for contractual regulation (Andersson and Moroni, 2014).

In short, the fundamental elements of certain traditional cities (in Europe) were the following: the spatially concentrated presence of various owners, incremental and open-ended development regulated by general and abstract local building codes (i.e. the possibility granted to households to constantly adapt and renovate their properties without setting a specific predetermined spatial end-state), and continuous adjustments over time among different parties (e.g. the possibilities for owners to adopt place-specific solutions after some agreement with their neighbours).

This process had two main virtues. Firstly, by adopting an incremental development largely based on small-scale propriety rights, it guaranteed the conservation of, and respect for, the existing built environment. Secondly, by allowing inhabitants to act on their property, it welcomed progressive additions and novelties resulting from the multiple decisions of different agents. Interestingly, these development principles are coherent with what in the complexity theories of cities is generally referred to as *dynamic stability* (Rauws, 2017; De Roo, 2018).

2.2.2 The impact of modern planning

The old codes regulating the evolution of certain traditional cities (e.g. in Europe and part of the Mediterranean area) were constituted mainly by *proscriptive* rules (i.e. prohibition: *thou shalt not* instead of *thou shalt*). These types of rules are profoundly different from modern land-use plans and building standards, which rely for a large part on the use of positive *prescriptions.* The peculiarity of proscriptive rules is that, given their negative nature, they cannot predefine or impose any predetermined social-spatial configurations. Instead, they mainly aim to avoid the emergence of certain nuisances produced by particular actions on other people's properties.

As the work of Besim Hakim (2014) demonstrates, the rules included in the old codes were mainly negative and general. They mostly dealt with matters such as privacy, accessibility to property, sunlight, smells, noise, safety issues. Given their abstract and general nature, the rules included in the old codes could accommodate the development of spontaneous configurations and ensure the possibility of creating unique urban settlements.[6]

By contrast, modern planning has generated an extensive use of positive prescriptions to establish functionally coordinated urban transformations.[7] The actions of different individuals (e.g. landowners, householders, builders) started to be regulated instrumentally to achieve the predetermined goals of comprehensive land-use plans. According to Marco Romano (2010: 99), the second half of the twentieth century was indeed a fertile period for national governments to impose the same planning criteria to all cities, introducing new architectural and morphological principles that replaced the longstanding, largely self-coordinating local systems and development practices. As argued by Jane Jacobs (1961), orthodox planning insistently tried to simplify the complexity of cities. To some extent, the foundations of the modern movement were mainly based on the rejection of complexity (Sennett, 1970).

This shift in urban history contributed to lowering the overall spontaneous character and adaptive capacity of many cities (that, for centuries, had guaranteed the evolution of unique places, e.g. in Europe) and made their development process more standardised (Hakim, 2014: 99). For example, it would be impossible today to recreate the same physical patterns of certain traditional cities and old towns due to the numerous rigid prescriptions regarding minimum road widths, minimum distances between buildings, minimum parking lots, minimum spaces for green areas, and other standards that reduce the agents' action space and, consequently, the capacity of the built environment to accommodate continuous adjustments. In short, the planning approach consolidated during the twentieth century widely neglected the adaptive and open-ended generative principles of the traditional city.

2.2.3 The influence of the neighbourhood-unit concept

With the affirmation of modern planning came also the spread of AANs. One of the triggering factors was the willingness to build self-sufficient neighbourhood units (Perry, 1929). As already highlighted, their construction did not occur without valid reasons. For example, after World War II, the demand for housing increased exponentially, and national states and local governments enacted planning policies to provide healthy dwellings.[8] However, if, on the one hand, AANs were the result of strong and urgent housing needs, on the other hand, they were the direct consequence of new urban, social and political ideologies aiming to develop top-down organised environments where residential, productive and commercial functions would be clearly distinguished and separated (Mehaffy, et al. 2015).

With this shift, the scale and frame of reference of planners changed. If, before the twentieth century, the main focus of planning had been the design of public spaces and infrastructures along with the introduction of building codes (Moroni, 2023), thereafter comprehensive large-scale development schemes and land-uses plans became the praxis (Lang, 2006). What once had been the incremental result of multiple actions of independent urban agents suddenly became the result of top-down and centrally coordinated plans. Public streets, once near to private properties and designed to facilitate access to them, started to be separated from buildings, changing the traditional relationship between public and private spaces in favour of ample, undefined, and often underused open areas. The typical small and demand-driven developments of the urban fabric, very popular before the twentieth century (e.g. in Europe), were abandoned in favour of large-scale supply-driven transformations (Swyngedouw et al., 2002; McGreevy, 2017).

Unfortunately, many scholars excluded from their analyses the way in which the traditional city had evolved. They focused almost exclusively on planning ideas that became mainstream during the twentieth century. Consequently, an essential heritage of practices and principles was almost entirely dissipated.

In planning theory and practice, attempts to rediscover past practices have recently been made. Evident cases are, for example, the many projects developed in recent years in accordance with the *New Urbanism* movement. However, a clear shortcoming of these projects is that most of them merely replicate the *forms* and *appearance* of the traditional city without considering its development *process*, which was not designed but emerged over time within the boundaries set by certain general rules and principles.

3 Discussion: An (anti)adaptability "detector"

Urban settlements can be complex and open to adaptations or, conversely, simple and resistant to change. This depends on (and is visible when looking at) the number and intensity of actions that shape and reshape the built environment. A simple configuration is usually an order that is deliberately designed. By contrast, a complex configuration has often an emergent character.[9] In short: Urban areas developed in a highly self-adaptive manner are usually complex, while anti-adaptive neighbourhoods are simple and overall static configurations.

Figure 5.4 presents eight characteristics that might help to differentiate adaptive from anti-adaptive neighbourhoods. These characteristics manifest not in a black-and-white manner but to different extents. Observe that not all of the features set out in Figure 5.4 must be present to classify a neighbourhood as adaptive or anti-adaptive. Sometimes, one specific feature is enough to compromise the adaptive capacity of an urban area. The schema can be used as a sort of "urban adaptability detector" with which to analyse existing urban contexts (e.g. to assess their degree of adaptability or the conditions constraining it) and as a general guide for designing or redesigning new settlements.[10]

Let us consider the eight factors in detail.

i Attractiveness. At least initially, AANs are usually quite attractive (e.g. to new dwellers). However, their level of attractiveness often decreases in the long run due to their incapacity to self-renovate and the difficulty of intervening in them.[11] By contrast, more adaptive settlements possess the "quality without a name", as Christopher Alexander (1980) puts it, that guarantees their survival, endurance and long-term attractiveness. This quality

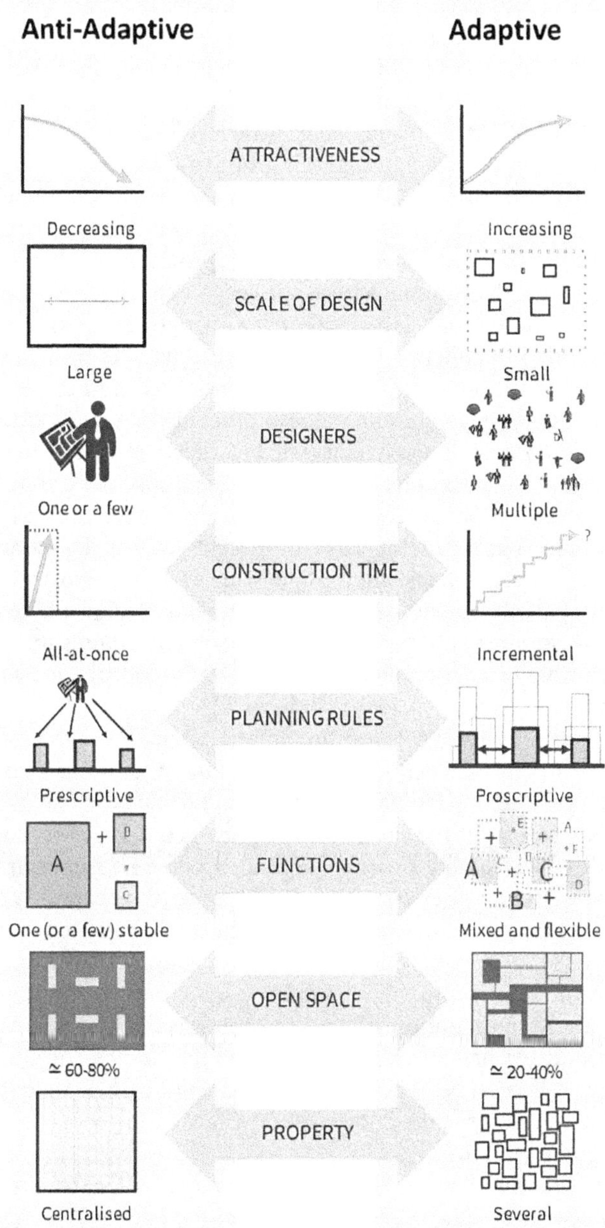

Figure 5.4 An "urban adaptability detector"

represents the encompassing life of the built environment and its ability to stimulate continuous adaptations and actions. Usually, given their open-ended nature and the uncertainty surrounding their incremental development, adaptable neighbourhoods are not very attractive during their early development phases. However, as they evolve – and given their intricacy and complexity – these urban areas can reach a high level of attractiveness.

ii The scale of design. AANs are often the product of comprehensive projects that extend spatial intervention over large areas, for instance, an entire neighbourhood; projects of this kind are approached like architectural projects expanded to the urban scale. In developing large-scale transformations, planners usually carry out preliminary operations to readjust the previously fragmented land ownership – which is considered a negative aspect – into a single compendium.[12] Developments of this kind are often considered economically efficient, but they can also cause serious problems. For example, they easily oversimplify the use of the city. Moreover, the larger the design scale, the higher the risk, also in economic terms, in the case of design failure. By contrast, in adaptive urban areas, the design scale is limited to the scale of single parcels and plots of land or crucial public spaces such as streets, squares and parks. This approach contributes to creating a more diverse environment that is centrally coordinated to only a minimal extent.

iii Designers. In AANs, the entire area is often conceived as a single design operation, defined in great detail by one designer or one specific group of designers collaborating to achieve the same goal. In this case, "all the design intelligence gets forced to the earliest part of the building process" (Brand, 1995: 63). Hence, in AANs, there is often a clear correspondence between one specific designer and the designed urban area (i.e. architect X designed neighbourhood Y). Conversely, in an adaptive built environment, it is impossible to identify any specific designer entirely responsible for the final configuration of the neighbourhood. An adaptive built environment has as many designers as the number of agents who shape it over time. The design responsibilities are, therefore, distributed among many subjects, not a few as in the case of AANs (Habraken, 2016).

iv Construction time. AANs are usually constructed from scratch and relatively quickly. Once their design is ready, the main problem is implementing it as soon as possible, so that almost no room is left for changes during and after the construction process.

All of this, in practice, may produce questionable effects and potential complications. For example, because these areas have been constructed all at once, they can undergo synchronous degradation processes after some years.[13] This phenomenon rarely occurs in adaptive built environments (Salingaros, 2018) because they are developed incrementally and comprise a differentiated building stock: that is, buildings of different ages, values, states of maintenance, and a more variegated mix of users. This situation reduces the risk of synchronous degradation processes and, potentially, offers more opportunities to fulfil the needs of different social groups while naturally creating more diversity and intricacy.

v Planning rules. A significant characteristic of AANs is that their physical configuration tends to coincide with detailed planning regulations and standards. In this way, crucial aspects such as density, building heights, in-between distances, percentage of public and private spaces, land uses and functions are frozen, leaving only little room for further development and adjustments (Manewa et al., 2016: 150). Planning rules are, in this case, highly prescriptive. By contrast, in adaptive built environments, planning rules do not coincide with the physical configuration. They leave enough room for further improvements and actions. Consequently, continual gradual change is possible and spontaneous diversification is probable.

vi Functions. AANs are prevalently mono-functional (or they comprise only a limited number of centrally defined functions). Sometimes, due to the almost exclusive presence of residential functions, AANs are not surprisingly considered to be "dormitories". Conversely, adaptive built environments are flexible, and they accommodate multiple uses that are also open to change. In these areas, ingenious adaptations for new uses are apparent in the stratification of different functions and their mixed and intricate interrelations;[14] the continuous mingling of people frequenting them for different purposes is usually a good signal. Jane Jacobs (1961) refers to this concept as *intricacy*, which is related to the variety of reasons for which people come to the neighbourhoods. Adaptive neighbourhoods usually exhibit a higher level of intricacy or, at least, can potentially accommodate it.[15]

vii Collective open space. A common characteristic of AANs is the vast amounts of open space usually managed by a single agency, for instance, the local municipality or a residential association. In AANs, the excessive presence of open spaces – often denigrated by being given the label of *no-man's-land* – may generate safety issues and problems of maintenance and control. Conversely, in the case of the traditional city, open and collectively managed spaces were usually created only in the case of strict necessity (Webster, 2007; Habraken, 2016). In complex and adaptive built environments, a large amount of land is usually built upon, while only a moderate amount of space is left open. By contrast, in many AANs, it is typical to have a large amount of land left open and unbuilt on (Jacobs, 1961: 214–215). Clearly, the presence of open spaces is not a problem in itself. Open and collectively accessible green areas, for example, may play a key role in improving the quality of local places and providing vital environmental amenities. However, a disproportionate presence of open spaces (e.g. parking lots, wide streets, underused green spaces) can easily diminish the vitality of contexts and decrease the *action space* potential.

viii Ownership system. AANs are frequently organised into very large forms of hybrid or collective ownership (Chapter 4) and present the same problems as anticommons do (Heller, 1998), as in the case of huge super-condominiums.[16] In this case, the salient parts of the buildings and open spaces are co-owned by multiple owners. In this way, dwellers' freedom to act and modify the uses of the buildings, or their appearance, is limited to their own apartments. To adapt the most significant aspects of an AAN, when possible, dwellers need to obtain the consent of large majorities and act collectively (Chen and Webster, 2005). This ownership situation has clear advantages (e.g. sharing certain costs and responsibilities), but it also discourages change and constrains the expression of individuals' creativity. Conversely, a crucial feature of adaptive built environments is the presence of many independent owners in a position to act directly and without intermediation. In this way, the functioning of urban areas depends on the decentralised responsibilities of several agents.[17]

4 Conclusion

This chapter has explored the differences between the typical traditional (adaptive) and the modern (anti-adaptive) built environment, as well as the process that brought about important shifts in the twentieth century. Moreover, it has discussed the main problems of AANs, their main characteristics, and the circumstances in which planners and designers are responsible for their creation and perpetuation.

Before some final remarks are made, it is necessary to underscore that it has not been the aim of this chapter to blame or negatively judge the existence of AANs in and of themselves. These areas play an important role for the many individuals living in them. The purpose of the discussion has been to emphasise those conditions from which an adaptive built environment can eventually arise. That said, if we recognise the importance of having neighbourhoods that are adaptable, a possible future challenge for planners and designers will be to recover and adapt some of the principles that marked the evolution of the traditional city.

From this perspective, crucial questions should primarily concern: (i) what actually needs to be designed on a large scale and what does not (e.g. Should planners design only the most important open spaces? If so, what kind of open spaces are important and how should they be designed?); (ii) the appropriate end-independent role of planning and building regulations; (iii) the presence of several owners in a position to act directly (as a pivotal factor in fostering diversity and the distribution of design responsibility).

The issue of regulation requires further specification (we will return extensively to this question in Chapter 7). However, here we can already state that contemporary discussion can be much enriched if more attention is paid to three factors usually ignored in the current debate: *action, ownership*, and *time*. Indeed, the main problem with AANs is not so much, as many planners and policymakers believe, the need for further centrally coordinated plans, investments and interventions intended to regenerate them, as the lack of flexible space for incremental long-term adaptations.[18]

Notes

1 See e.g. Harris (2011) and Alfasi et al. (2020).
2 See e.g. Banerjee and Baer (1984), Rofé (1995), Johnson (2002), Lawhon (2009), Rohe (2009), Mehaffy et al. (2015).
3 In this regard, an interesting perspective is put forward by Brand (1995).
4 See e.g. Levy (1999), Lang (2006), Alfasi et al. (2020).
5 See e.g. Helleman and Wassenberg (2004), Rowlands et al. (2009), Zarecor (2011), Hirt (2013) and Webb and Webber (2017).
6 The example of Kreuzviertel (Dortmund) included in the book's Annex confirms what Hakim (2014) argues. Developed starting from the late nineteenth century, the neighbourhood has evolved primarily based on very simple rules, mostly of a negative nature, mainly focused on avoiding the production of certain undesired externalities or, more simply, coordinating certain general aspects such as building alignment.
7 See e.g. Alfasi and Portugali (2007), Alfasi (2018).
8 See e.g. Turkington et al. (2004), Rowlands et al. (2009).

9 On the trade-off between design and complexity, see Moroni (2010b, 2011), Kelso et al. (2016), Ikeda (2017). Cozzolino (2018) and Debray et al. (2023).

10 This schema is the result of years of analyses and studies, which have also been included in some curricula of MSc students in planning and design faculties to help guide their analytical work on understanding urban dynamics and the openness of certain urban areas to long-term adaptability. As far as we know, the "(anti)adaptability detector" is currently used in courses at RWTH Aachen, Groningen University, the Polytechnic University of Milan, Tel-Aviv University, and Ben-Gurion University of the Negev. It has also been included in the third edition of the compendium on urban design and public space by Carmona (2021). An interesting study which seeks to operationalise this schema is Tsahor et al. (2023). For further developments, see also Carter and Moroni (2022).

11 See e.g. Rowlands et al. (2009) and Webb and Webber (2017).

12 See Lin (2005), Louw (2008) and Kilić et al. (2019). In opposing land fragmentation, Sternberg (2000: 274) maintains that "individual property owners cannot – through the atomised market process alone – shape the meanings of the urban whole".

13 See Kabisch and Grossmann (2013) and Webb and Webber (2017).

14 Jacobs (1961: 194) presents this idea when she describes the complexity of a poor but highly vibrant neighbourhood: "The town-house parlor that becomes a craftsman's showroom, […] the basement […] becomes an immigrants' club, the garage or brewery […] becomes a theater, […] the warehouse […] becomes a factory for Chinese food […]". These are the kinds of minor changes continuously occurring in response to evolving human needs. This is not only an enjoyable phenomenon; it also fulfils a practical need guaranteeing the survival of buildings.

15 As regards the number, types and distribution of functions, it is crucial to stress that planning can only create certain *conditions* (e.g. certain rules or incentives: Moroni and Cozzolino, 2020) that welcome the presence of a variety of different uses; they cannot directly provide them (as we will see better in Chapter 7). The point is that most of the functions that make a neighbourhood vibrant (e.g. bars, restaurants and shops) are the result of market processes and the interplay of multiple factors that can be only partially controlled by planners (Moroni, 2010a; Holcombe, 2013; Bertaud, 2018). To put it differently, planning cannot force private individuals to run certain businesses if entrepreneurs do not want to do so. Neither can public institutions, such as local governments, provide all of the functions a neighbourhood needs to become vibrant.

16 See Morris and West (2003), Renae Johnston and Reid (2013) and Webb and Webber (2017).

17 This situation has positive aspects, in line with Brand's (1995: 173) observation that "small groups adapt more quickly than large groups".

18 In this regard, an interesting question concerns the future of the old historic urban areas (e.g. in Italy) which visually express their self-adaptive and incremental development process. Due to recent, rigid preservation policies and restrictive rules, these areas sometimes present the problems typical of an AAN. An intriguing research question is whether and to what extent preservation policies can be reconciled with the necessity of long-term adaptability.

References

Akbar, J. (1988). *Crisis in the Built Environment: The Case of the Muslim City.* Singapore: Concept Media Pte Ltd.

Alexander, C. (1979). *The Timeless Way of Building*, vol. I. New York: Oxford University Press.

Alexander, C. (1980). *The Nature of Order: The Process of Creating Life.* London: Routledge, 2002.

Alfasi, N. (2018). The coding turn in urban planning: Could it remedy the essential drawbacks of planning? *Planning Theory*, 17 (3): 375–395.

Alfasi, N., Portugali, J. (2007). Planning rules for a self-planned city. *Planning Theory*, 6 (2): 164–182.

Alfasi, N., Shnizik, A.R., Davidson, M., Kahani, A. (2020). Anti-adaptive urbanism: Long-term implications of building inward-turned neighborhoods in Israel. *Journal of Urbanism: International Research on Placemaking and Urban Sustainability*, 13 (4): 387–409.

Andersson, D.E., Moroni, S. (eds.) (2014). *Cities and Private Planning. Property Rights, Entrepreneurship and Transaction Costs.* Cheltenham: Edward Elgar.

Banerjee, T., Baer, W.C. (1984). *Beyond the Neighborhood Unit: Residential Environments and Public Policy.* New York: Plenum Press.

Blandy, S., Dupuis, A., Dixon, J.E. (eds) (2010). *Multi-Owned Housing: Law, Power and Practice.* Farnham: Ashgate.

Bertaud, A. (2018). *Order without Design. How Markets Shape Cities.* Cambridge, MA: MIT Press.

Brand, S. (1995). *How Buildings Learn: What Happens after They're Built.* London: Penguin.

Carmona, M. (2021). *Public Places Urban Spaces. The Dimensions of Urban Design.* New York: Routledge.

Carter, I., Moroni, S. (2022). Adaptive and anti-adaptive neighbourhoods: Investigating the relationship between individual choice and systemic adaptability. *Environment and Planning B*, 49 (2): 722–736.

Chen, S.C., Webster, C.J. (2005). Homeowners associations, collective action and the costs of private governance. *Housing Studies*, 20 (2): 205–220.

Cozzolino, S. (2018). Reconsidering spontaneity and flexibility after Jane Jacobs. How do they work under different kind of planning conditions? *Cosmos+Taxis*, 5 (3/4): 14–24.

Debray, H., Kraff, N.J., Zhu, X.X., Taubenböck, H. (2023). Planned, unplanned, or in-between? A concept of the intensity of plannedness and its empirical relation to the built urban landscape across the globe. *Landscape and Urban Planning*, 233: 1–27.

De Roo, G. (2018). Ordering principles in a dynamic world of change. On social complexity, transformation and the conditions for balancing purposeful interventions and spontaneous change. *Progress in Planning*, 125: 1–32.

Habraken, N.J. (1998). *The Structure of the Ordinary: Form and Control in the Built Environment.* Cambridge, MA: The MIT Press.

Habraken, N.J. (2016). Cultivating complexity: The need for a shift in cognition. In J. Portugali, E. Stolk (eds), *Complexity, Cognition, Urban Planning and Design*. Berlin: Springer, 55–74.

Hakim, B.S. (2014). *Mediterranean Urbanism*. Berlin: Springer.

Harris, D.C. (2011). Condominium and the city: The rise of property in Vancouver. *Law & Social Inquiry*, 36 (3): 694–726.

Hayek, F.A. (1945). The use of knowledge in society. *The American Economic Review*, 35 (4): 519–530.

Helleman, G., Wassenberg, F. (2004). The renewal of what was tomorrow's idealistic city. Amsterdam's Bijlmermeer high-rise. *Cities*, 21 (1): 3–17.

Heller, M.A. (1998). The tragedy of the anticommons: Property in the transition from Marx to markets. *Harvard Law Review*, 111 (3): 621–688.

Hirt, S. (2013). Whatever happened to the (post) socialist city? *Cities*, 32 (1): 29–38.

Holcombe, R.G. (2013). Planning and the invisible hand: Allies or adversaries? *Planning Theory*, 12 (2): 199–210.

Ikeda, S (2017). The city cannot be a work of art. *Cosmos+Taxis*, 4 (2): 79–86.

Jacobs, J (1961). *The Death and Life of Great American Cities*. New York: Random House.

Johnson, D.L. (2002). Origin of the Neighbourhood Unit. *Planning Perspectives*, 17 (3): 227–245.

Kabisch, S., Grossmann, K. (2013). Challenges for large housing estates in light of population decline and ageing: Results of a long-term survey in East Germany. *Habitat International*, 39: 232–239.

Kelso, J.S., Stolk, E., Portugali, J. (2016). Self-organisation and design as a complementary pair. In J. Portugali, E. Stolk (eds), *Complexity, Cognition, Urban Planning and Design*. Berlin: Springer, 43–53.

Kilić, J., Jajac, N., Rogulj, K., Mastelić-Ivić, S. (2019). Assessing land fragmentation in planning sustainable urban renewal. *Sustainability*, 11 (9): 1–24.

Lang, J. (2006). *Urban Design*. London: Routledge.

Lawhon, L. (2009). The neighborhood unit: physical design or physical determinism? *Journal of Planning History*, 8 (2): 111–132.

Levy, A. (1999). Urban morphology and the problem of the modern urban fabric: some questions for research. *Urban Morphology*, 3: 79–85.

Lin, T.C. (2005). Land assembly in a fragmented land market through land readjustment. *Land Use Policy*, 22 (2): 95–102.

Louw, E. (2008). Land assembly for urban transformation. The case of 's-Hertogenbosch in The Netherlands. *Land Use Policy*, 25 (1): 69–80.

Manewa, A., Siriwardena, M., Ross, A., Madanayake, U. (2016). Adaptable buildings for sustainable built environment. *Built Environment Project and Asset Management*, 6 (2): 139–158.

McGreevy, M.P. (2017). Complexity as the telos of postmodern planning and design: Designing better cities from the bottom-up. *Planning Theory*, 17 (3): 355–374.

Mehaffy, M.W., Porta, S., Romice, O. (2015). The "neighborhood unit" on trial: A case study in the impacts of urban morphology. *Journal of*

Urbanism: International Research on Placemaking and Urban Sustainability, 8 (2): 199–217.

Moroni, S. (2010a). Rethinking the theory and practice of land-use regulation: Towards nomocracy. *Planning Theory*, 9 (2): 137–155.

Moroni, S. (2010b). An evolutionary theory of institutions and a dynamic approach to reform. *Planning Theory*, 9 (4): 275–297.

Moroni, S. (2011). The role of deliberate intervention on organizations and institutions: A response to Alexander. *Planning Theory*, 10 (2): 190–197.

Moroni, S. (2023). Distinguishing "planning" from the "plan". Institutional and professional implications of taking urban complexity seriously. *European Planning Studies*, 31 (11): 2327–2341.

Moroni, S., Cozzolino, S. (2020). Actions and conditions of actions. In G. de Roo, C. Yamu, C. Zuidema (eds), *Handbook on Planning and Complexity*. Cheltenham: Edward Elgar, 186–202.

Morris, E.M., West, M.D. (2003). The tragedy of the condominiums: Legal responses to collective action problems after the Kobe earthquake. *American Journal of Comparative Law*, 4: 903–940.

Perry, C.A. (1929). The Neighborhood Unit: A scheme of arrangement for the family life community. In Committee on Regional Plan of New York and Its Environs, A Regional Plan for New York and Its Environs. New York.

Pirenne, H. (1927). Les villes du Moyen Age. Bruxelles: Maurice Lamertin. English translation: *Medieval Cities*. Princeton: Princeton University Press, 2014.

Rauws, W. (2017). Embracing uncertainty without abandoning planning: Exploring an adaptive planning approach for guiding urban transformations. *DisP-The Planning Review*, 53 (1): 32–45.

Renae Johnston, N., Reid, S. (2013). Multi-owned developments: a life cycle review of a developing research area. *Property Management*, 31 (5): 366–388.

Rofé, Y. (1995). Space and community: The spatial foundations of urban neighborhoods. *Berkeley Planning Journal*, 10: 107–125.

Rohe, W.M. (2009). From local to global: One hundred years of neighborhood planning. *Journal of the American Planning Association*, 75 (2): 209–230.

Romano, M. (2010). *Ascesa e declino della città europea*. Milano: Cortina.

Rowlands, R., Musterd, S., Van Kempen, R. (2009). *Mass Housing in Europe: Multiple Faces of Development, Change and Response*. London: Palgrave Macmillan.

Salingaros, N.A. (2018). Adaptive versus random complexity. *New Design Ideas*, 2 (2): 51–61.

Sennett, R. (1970). *The Uses of Disorder: Personal Identity and City Life*. New York: Knopf.

Sternberg, E. (2000). An integrative theory of urban design. *Journal of the American Planning Association*, 66 (3): 265–278.

Swyngedouw, E., Moulaert, F., Rodriguez, A. (2002). Neoliberal urbanisation in Europe: Large-scale urban development projects and the new urban policy. *Antipode*, 34 (3): 542–577.

Tsahor, M., Katoshevski-Cavari, R., Alfasi, N. (2023). Assessing urban adaptability: The key is in the land use plan. *Land Use Policy*, 126, 1–11.

Tunstall, R. (2016). Are neighbourhoods dynamic or are they slothful? The limited prevalence and extent of change in neighbourhood socio-economic status, and its implications for regeneration policy. *Urban Geography*, 37 (5): 769–784.

Turkington, R., Van Kempen, R., Wassenberg, F. (2004). *High-Rise Housing in Europe: Current Trends and Future Prospects.* Delft: Delft University Press.

Webb, B., Webber, S. (2017). The implications of condominium neighbourhoods for long-term urban revitalisation. *Cities*, 61: 48–57.

Webster, C. (2007). Property rights, public space and urban design. *Town Planning Review*, 78 (1): 81–101.

Zarecor, K.E. (2011). Socialist neighborhoods after socialism: The past, present, and future of postwar housing in the Czech Republic. *East European Politics and Societies*, 26 (3): 486–509.

6 Beauty

1 Introduction

Today, beauty is a marginal topic within the scientific debate on cities. Fundamental questions such as "What constitutes urban beauty?", "What are its origins?", "How can planners and designers contribute to its creation?", and "How did the urban areas that we find appealing evolve?", largely remain unexplored. Neglecting these issues fails to serve the interests of both citizens and planners.

This chapter considers two principal hypotheses. First, a superficial consensus on a vague and unsatisfactory conception of urban beauty hinders substantive discussion. Second, including also the issues of *action* and *complexity* in the discourse provides better understanding of the unique characteristics of urban beauty.

From this perspective, the chapter first briefly examines the general concept of beauty and its application. It then highlights key features to be considered when discussing urban beauty. The findings of the analysis reveal necessary conceptual changes and possible new approaches. Before starting, it is important to reiterate that the topic of the chapter is *urban* beauty: the attractiveness of the urbanised and dense settings typical of cities.

2 Focus: Revisiting the concept

2.1 The concept of beauty

The concept of beauty, which is the focus of a significant body of philosophical discourse, is applicable to numerous fields (e.g. literature, theatre, architecture, painting) and aspects of life (e.g. landscapes, machines, human bodies). When discussing the universal meaning of beauty, Umberto Eco (2004) argues that "beautiful" is an adjective

DOI: 10.4324/9781003454304-6

that we use to denote something that complies with certain ideal principles and that we find pleasing for what it is, regardless of whether or not we use/own it. For example, person X thinks that building Y is beautiful because it invokes (and adheres to) a certain ideal of beauty W, even though person X does not live therein or nearby, nor has any meaningful connection to it.

Beauty has always represented a fundamental ideal (Eco, 2004; Scruton, 2007, 2021; Chiodo, 2017, 2019). While beauty has usually been linked to universal principles,[1] experience of it depends also on how individuals perceive and appreciate the world. Indeed, beauty is a form of pleasure connected to individuals' cognitive understanding (Armstrong and Detweiler-Bedell, 2008; Skov and Nadal, 2021).

2.2 A concept in crisis

The concept of beauty is usually perceived as elusive and ambiguous for several reasons. Examining the significant conceptual transformation that has occurred within this concept reveals intriguing aspects.

The central aspect of the old concept of beauty was the recognition of a harmonious whole to which individuals could elevate themselves, and become part of, through their actions and works. In this sense, beauty was a sort of "overarching feature". Aspiring to beauty meant, first and foremost, trying to be part of, and participate in, a complex and superior form of order (Stolnitz, 1961). To quote Carleton Noyes (1907: 183): "Where the spirit of man comes into harmony with a harmony external to it, there is beauty".

The concept of beauty started to change during the nineteenth century, when the individual artistic act gradually replaced the intersubjective pursuit of beauty. With the rise of new artistic movements, the aspiration to beauty became more *self-referential*, provoking a fundamental cultural change: from aspiring to be part of a higher harmony and complex whole to creating unique works of art (Shiner, 2003). Twentieth-century avant-gardes consolidated this change through a search for *endless novelties* which led to a progressive relativisation of the concept and the loss of reference points. In this way, in the modern and contemporary ages, the pursuit of beauty mainly took the form of artistic gestures and provocative attitudes (Bodei, 1995; Vercellone, 2008).

In short, according to the old concept of beauty, the central role is played by the harmonious relationship of an action and/or an object with and within a "broader whole". In the subsequent and contemporary concept, the major role is instead assumed by the ability of an artist to create unique works of art able to evoke certain reactions in observers. In the latter case, the pursuit of beauty gives prominence to the artist. As we will see, such a cultural and conceptual change impacted the understanding of *good urban design* as well.

2.3 Its application in urban design and planning

Emily Talen and Cliff Ellis (2002: 38) observe that "beauty seems to have almost vanished in the literature". Nowadays, the topic emerges only sporadically in urban studies, and when it does, its conceptualisation seems to be rather ambiguous.[2] The debate on what urban beauty is, how it emerges, and the role of planning in its creation is almost absent even though beauty is a crucial aspect of citizens' everyday lives. Indeed, how people perceive beauty affects their well-being and engagement with their surroundings. In short, beauty substantially impacts people's lives.[3]

Most scholars consider urban beauty to be so inherently subjective that it is preferable to keep it out of scientific debates.[4] This does not mean that planners have not dealt with the concept of urban beauty at all.[5] For a long time in the twentieth century, planning and design theories promoted an ideal of urban beauty based on formalistic aspects of the built environment: normative ideas of beauty concerning the architectural spatial and visual configuration have prevailed (Lang, 2006).[6] According to Nigel Taylor (2009), conventional and widespread concepts of urban beauty are closely linked to specific notions of *good design*, placing a clear organisation of the built environment at the heart of the discourse.[7]

In brief, the concept of urban beauty, consolidated during the twentieth century and still prevailing nowadays, largely embraces the idea of the city as *a work of art*: that is, an idea which implies that planners and designers can intentionally and directly create urban beauty by focusing almost exclusively on the shape and appearance of the built environment. This approach to urban beauty gives planners and designers prime responsibility for developing and generating forms of designed orders.[8]

From this perspective, the approach to *urban* beauty is similar to that of *architectural* beauty, with the difference that, in the former case, the object (i.e. the "urban") expands in scale.

An interesting aspect is that, as in the case of the crisis of the general concept of beauty, with the affirmation of modern and post-modern design movements also the concept of urban beauty has become more self-referential and subjective, giving prominence to the design acts of *archistars* on a large-scale.[9]

2.4 Implications for theory and practice

This understanding of good design (and beauty) has two components: on the one hand, the appreciation of urban areas manifesting forms of designed order (that is, places that are, so to speak, well-designed); on the other hand, and complimentarily, the disdain for chaotic and disordered areas lacking design coordination (Slaev et al., 2022). A further possibility, taking into consideration the original concept of beauty – that is, the appreciation of a more complex and self-organising form of urban order – is generally not considered. In other words, serious debates on the possibility of a sense of beautiful wholeness that is not, in a strict sense, designed is marginal. Well-known exceptions include the works of Christopher Alexander (1979, 1980): consider his concepts of "quality without a name", "adaptational complexity" and "living structure".

To date, besides a small group of scholars who remain relatively marginal, an understanding of urban beauty of this kind – which is more coherent with the old concept of beauty – is still underrated.[10] As Christopher Alexander (2021: 229) writes: "The beauty of naturally occurring patterns and forms is rarely discussed by scientists".

A major problem is that, inevitably, the contemporary attitude encourages the creation of out-of-context projects characterised by the large-scale exaltation of the creative flair of designers. This attitude induces designers to conceive development projects as *closed* systems that are not open to self-adaptive processes of change. Indeed, current mainstream urban design practices can hardly imagine open-ended, slow, and self-adaptive transformations created over time by a multiplicity of urban agents. On the contrary, common practices rely on the design of large areas, with the tendency to over-define their physical and spatial features regardless of the scale of reference of the different urban and architectural elements.[11] A direct consequence is also that design projects do not often prioritise the design of the public layout (e.g. streets, squares) over that of buildings. Indeed, the design of buildings frequently predominates over that of public spaces – an approach that conflicts with the basic purpose of urban design.[12]

This tendency is also apparent in university degree courses in planning and design. Students often learn how to design comprehensive masterplans and exceptional architectural landmarks but they fail to focus on the design of the ordinary urban fabric, nor do they investigate what kind of urban areas people really appreciate and why, or how these areas have emerged over time and what conditions have enabled their long-term survival. From the outset, students approach urban projects as self-standing works of art, disconnected from the complexity of urban realities.[13] This makes it difficult for them to develop an appropriate level of sensitivity and learn how to relate their interventions to the existing urban order.

2.5 Reopening the discourse

The urban beauty discourse is certainly not central in contemporary scientific debates.[14] Although some authors consider the topic to be elitist,[15] experiencing the beautifulness of urban settings positively affects people regardless of their social status. However, the way in which the concept of beauty has evolved over time, transitioning from a desire to contribute to the harmony of the existing order to the creation of self-standing works of art, does not help in approaching the issue. We think that the contemporary conception of urban beauty has significant limitations; paradoxically, as argued by Marco Romano (2008 and 2010), this concept may contribute to diminishing the proper beauty of cities.

3 Discussion: Three overlooked characteristics

One of the main obstacles in discussing urban beauty is not having sufficiently reflected on what its characteristics are and how they make urban beauty different from other types of beauty. To make progress in this field of inquiry, it is crucial to specify what is being talked about. In this regard, rediscovering the old concept of beauty and integrating it with the notion of complexity opens interesting scenarios. For this purpose, three questions must be addressed:

- i What kind of object are we referring to when we discuss urban beauty? What is its genesis? Can urban beauty be a work of art?
- ii What experiential information comes into play when we judge urban beauty? Is it only visual, or do inputs of other kinds play an important role as well?
- iii What role does perceptual complexity play? Can complexity increase aesthetic appreciation? In what circumstances?

3.1 First point: An urban system is not a simple (designed) object

Firstly, it is important to distinguish between aesthetic judgments concerning *one object* and those that concern *an ensemble of independent objects* (all of them together forming an emergent configuration).

Because of the contemporary and prevailing concept of beauty, it is common to think of beauty as a feature of a work of art and, therefore, to pass judgement on a finite and distinguishable designed object. While this approach is applicable in many cases – for instance, in those of a car, a boat, a sculpture, or a building – it runs into difficulties when it has to deal with open and complex systems like a city or parts of it.

In the case of works of art, artists can create and compose objects as they please; object forms, shapes, and harmonic appearances are all under their direct control. A city, however, cannot function in this manner. As Jane Jacobs (1961: 372) succinctly observes: "A city cannot be a work of art". In discussing this issue, she emphasises that a city is not under the control of a single actor (or artist); rather, it is an emergent living organism composed of multiple, diverse individuals who continuously and actively participate in its never-ending modification and evolution. Therefore, a city is not a simple object but instead a dynamic, ever-changing system composed of multiple objects continuously being created and adapted by numerous agents.

The crucial difference is that, when judging the aesthetic quality of single objects, one considers items intentionally created by specific agents with specific aesthetic canons in mind. Conversely, the city as a whole is for the large part a spontaneous system emerging from an uncountable number of actions in which multiple design interventions follow one another and are stratified. Despite planners' intentions, the city as a whole does not have a specific purpose or an intentional aesthetic canon; instead, inevitably, it expresses emerging properties, including aesthetic dimensions (Romano, 2008 and 2010).

Having highlighted this crucial difference, it is now important to stress that urban beauty, despite its emergent nature, does not come into existence through the simple aggregation of single and independently beautiful objects. As Mirza Tursić (2019: 212) notes, the aesthetic appreciation of a city "cannot be solely understood as the sum of the aesthetic appreciations of its separate parts". In other words, a sum of beautiful buildings does not necessarily generate a beautiful city. Actually (and quite frequently), even an ensemble of anonymous buildings can generate a pleasant urban area. Therefore, in discussing the beauty of one object (e.g. a building or a bridge) and an ensemble of multiple independent objects (e.g. an urban area composed of multiple building and structures owned by various agents), two distinct types of beauty (largely intentional/designed vs. largely unintentional/spontaneous) are at stake. Those who fail to recognise this difference risk falling into the trap of judging the beauty of a city as if it were a work of art despite the fact that a city is a dynamic, largely self-forming, living system. As Jane Jacobs (1961: 373) writes, "to approach a city as if it is a larger architectural problem [...] is to make the mistake of attempting to substitute art for life".[16]

In conclusion, urban beauty can be largely understood as an emerging property. The judgement that object X in city Y is beautiful (e.g. one building) is profoundly different from the judgement that the city/urban area Y is beautiful. The referential space, scale and genesis of X and Y are fundamentally different. The beauty of a building is (mainly) designed; that of a city is (mainly) emergent.

3.2 Second point: Urban beauty is not only material and visual

Secondly, the aesthetic appreciation of an urban area does not derive only from its material and physical appearance. A city is an interrelated socio-spatial whole, and so too is its beauty. The experience of beauty in the urban realm is multisensorial. It involves, for example, smells, sounds, people's behaviour, and street culture (De Franco and Moroni, 2023). If we reduce the understanding of urban beauty to a mere compositional architectonic notion, we focus only on one of the many aspects of the urban experience and ignore many other essential elements. In other words, urban beauty is not solely a material phenomenon; it is a more complex experience that interrelates social facts and the built environment. Some elements are visible and tangible, while others are not (Jorgensen, 2011).

This important point opens a completely new perspective on the concept of urban beauty. Indeed, not even Christopher Alexander – the most influential scholar in the tradition of combining complexity, cognitive science and aesthetics – clarified how social and intangible aspects impact beauty.[17]

Let us use the emblematic case of Venice as an example to reflect on this point. If Venice's beauty depends merely on the shape and form of the built environment, it should be feasible to recreate it. Indeed, some attempts to recreate Venice's physical appearance have been made worldwide, but the beauty of these places is incomparable to that of the real Venice.[18] The point is that urban beauty is something more profound than the form and shape of the built environment. It includes aspects that cannot be designed and are instead rooted in a cultural environment (e.g. how people interact in the streets and their dinnertime routines). Moreover, urban beauty results from long processes. Although its experience is limited to the present, time and *genius loci* – that is, the emergent process of creation and the frameworks behind its development – are unique elements that play a fundamental role in the formation of urban beauty and are difficult to control.[19]

Recent research conducted in Dortmund (Germany) has demonstrated that urban beauty depends significantly on aspects that do not necessarily concern the built environment *per se*. The study (see Annex) explored the characteristics of Kreuzviertel, one of the most appreciated neighbourhoods in the city. The study discovered that besides the shape and forms of the built environment (e.g. the style of building facades), a vital part of people's aesthetic judgments depended on the appreciation of the local lifestyle, the types of stores and businesses on the ground floor and the people frequenting the area. Moreover, the comparison of Kreuzviertel with Nordstadt (another neighbourhood in Dortmund built in the same period, ca. 1880–1930, with a similar urban fabric and street layout but a profoundly different social reputation) showed the crucial contribution of social aspects to the definition of "beauty". Although the two neighbourhoods have similar built environments, most people point to Kreuzviertel as more beautiful mainly because of its social characteristics.

Although only briefly presented here, the examples of Venice and Dortmund show that, in understanding urban beauty, there are no compositional and morphological aspects that *solely in themselves* can explain beauty. A city is an interconnected whole, and so too is its beauty. The aesthetic experience of the urban environment intrinsically includes physical, social and multisensorial aspects. Strictly speaking, only some of these elements are designable and tangible; and this is the reason why, recurrently, urban areas with no apparent morphological and architectural significance may be considered pleasant and beautiful if they possess certain non-formal qualities (e.g. when they express a specific culture: consider certain popular neighbourhoods in Berlin or London, for example). Conversely, well-designed urban environments with acknowledged morphological and architectural quality may be made unattractive by the presence of certain social dynamics (e.g. delinquency, poor hygienic conditions, poor maintenance) or the absence of others (for example, when an area is inexpressive or dull, as in the case of many anti-adaptive-neighbourhoods: Chapter 5).

3.3 Third point: Complexity increases aesthetic appreciation

A third important aspect of the aesthetic experience of cities and urban areas is the role of multiple stimuli as perceived by agents.

Studies in cognitive science and psychology have demonstrated that complex, apparently chaotic, environmental stimuli play an important role in aesthetic appreciation. Thomas Armstrong and Brian Detweiler-Bedell (2008: 308) write: "A mild aesthetic pleasure reliably accompanies the experience of simple stimuli [while] a more exhilarated form of aesthetic pleasure may accompany the experience of more complex stimuli". These findings have interesting implications for the understanding of urban beauty.

On placing action and complexity at the centre of the discussion, it is possible to differentiate between simple and complex urban areas according to the number of actions that have influenced their evolution and current dynamics.[20] In short, a complex urban environment is shaped by several urban agents; conversely, a simple environment is static and does not stimulate actions and interactions. For example, the vibrant city centre of Naples is a complex environment, while the TU Dortmund University campus is a simple one. The former is an intricate concentration of stimuli and the long-term product of the stratification of an uncountable number of actions; the latter is a calm environment, with scant stimuli, resulting from a single and comprehensive master plan. One can appreciate the design of the TU Dortmund University campus, but the Neapolitan urban environment has the potential to overwhelm the observer.[21] Cognitive scientists know very well why this is so.[22]

In this regard, cognitive science studies on aesthetic stimuli identify complexity as the variety and quantity of information and elements existing in a specific system.[23] The greater their variety and quantity, the greater the complexity of a particular system.[24] However, multiplicity alone is not enough to generate beauty. What enhances the aesthetic experience is the co-presence of complexity and certain discernible patterns.[25] As Rudolf Arnheim (1966: 124) writes: "Complexity without order produces confusion [and] order without complexity causes boredom".[26] The principle of *unity in variety* well summarises these conclusions.[27]

The findings of cognitive science provide important insights into understanding how complexity influences aesthetic experience, but they also highlight the importance of the presence of patterns in establishing an overall sense of harmony. This aspect is crucial because the urban experience is a *total* one. It involves not only architectural patterns but also other ones, for example, behavioural patterns. This viewpoint opens innovative spaces of discussion on the issue of urban beauty because, as observed in previous chapters of this book, most social-spatial patterns emerge and evolve spontaneously and cannot be directly controlled.

4 Conclusion

The discourse on urban beauty needs to be integrated with complexity thinking. The city is a complex system, and its aesthetic experience cannot but be *total*, meaning that the appreciation or otherwise of urban areas derives from multiple kinds of inputs, not only physical and visual ones. Moreover, complexity increases aesthetic appreciation provided that there exist certain discernible patterns. In this sense, and differently from widespread and contemporary beliefs, urban beauty radically differs from architectural beauty. The *object*, its *genesis* and *dynamics* are totally different.

Morphological and physical aspects are, of course, important in defining urban beauty, but they are insufficient for the purpose. A crucial point is that an essential component of the urban setting is "its life", that is, the continuous actions and interactions of individuals, local culture, and various social dynamics. It is reductive, if not impossible, to talk about urban beauty while excluding this component.

In this regard, the rediscovery of the old concept of beauty offers a promising scenario. It suggests that urban beauty cannot be directly created. Nevertheless, understanding how planning may contribute to urban beauty remains a challenging issue. If we accept the proposed perspective, planners should focus mainly on the provision of general frameworks that (i) on the one hand, hold the system together (thanks to simple basic rules regarding, for example, certain main aspects such as building street alignment and the provision of appropriately arranged public spaces and main infrastructure), and, on the other (ii) simultaneously grant ample space for the emergence of social-spatial diversity and complexity. In this regard, it is of key importance to consider that the planning framework can only facilitate the emergence of diversity because it will eventually emerge thanks to widespread actions and interactions of urban agents.[28]

Notes

1 Beauty possesses an intersubjective significance: Specific aesthetic canons – depending on cultural, geographical, and historical aspects – exert influence on and frame how individuals judge and experience beauty. Nasar (1988), for example, claims that patterns of cultural preference affect the aesthetic perception of places.

2 On the basis of critical findings in cognitive science, Carr (2022: 606), for example, maintains that "beauty cannot be read in an 'ordinary' or 'everyday' manner". Skov and Nadal (2021: 46) argue that the same person can find the same stimulus beautiful on one occasion but not on another. Ryser (2022: 21) raises the question of whether the "one-size-fits-

all concept of beauty is desirable or even conceivable". In short, despite its importance, the definition of beauty remains largely elusive.

3 On this, see Saito (2007), Hillman (2018), Skov and Nadal (2021).

4 For example, Hoch (2006: 368) maintains that "the influential method of experimental scientific inquiry relegates emotions and feelings to an inferior role in human judgment".

5 Among the many first influential "seeders" were Camillo Sitte (1889), Le Corbusier (1923), and Frank Lloyd Wright (1935). These authors had a great impact on treatment of the concept. A more recent example is Daniel Burnham with his ideas for the *City Beautiful Movement* (Wilson 1994), but also the well-known work by Lynch (1981).

6 See, for example, the recent and interesting report by the British Ministry of Housing, Communities & Local Government, *Living with beauty: promoting health, well-being and sustainable growth*, which deals with principles to promote and increase the use of high-quality design for new build homes and neighbourhoods (https://assets.publishing.service.gov.uk/government/uploads/system/uploads/attachment_data/file/861832/Living_with_beauty_BBBBC_report.pdf: accessed August 2023).

7 Specifically, the author argues that these ideas stem from a misinterpretation of Lynch's exploration of the spatial legibility concept. Taylor (2009: 189) notes that "the idea that legibility is an important indicator of the perceptible quality of townscapes, and therefore of good urban design, has been accepted by many urban design and planning theorists since Kevin Lynch's seminal work [...] The concept of legibility as a principle of (good) urban design, although important, is generally overrated. [...] Legibility *on its own* is not necessarily a significant criterion of the perceptible quality of townscapes"; therefore, "legibility *in itself* is not an important consideration or 'principle' of urban design". This aspect is also emphasised by Akkerman (2000: 272).

8 It is important to emphasise that the planning discourse during the first half of the twentieth century was primarily concentrated on developing models of desirable urbanism and city shapes (Taylor, 1999). The postwar planning approaches also focused on planning and decision-making processes (Moroni, 2019).

9 See on this Swyngedouw et al. (2002), McGreevy (2017), Alexander (2021). On the topic of *archistars*, see also Ponzini (2011) and Palermo and Ponzini (2012).

10 An interesting initiative is the *Building Beauty Program*, which takes place yearly in Sorrento, Naples (www.buildingbeauty.org/; accessed August 2023). See also Rofè et al. (2020).

11 The famous quote from the 1950s, "From the spoon to the city" by Rogers (1946), well represents this approach. See e.g. Cecchetti and Baker (2011).

12 See on this Biddulph (2012); Sternberg (2000); Cozzolino et al. (2020).

13 Alexander (2021: 213) clearly warned about the risks of an approach of this kind: "If everyone is trying to do something different [self-referential], then of course there will be chaos; just, indeed, what we have experienced in modern urbanism".

14 However, there is now renewed attention to the theme of beauty. For example, there are studies focused on beauty as a "form (or instrument) of justice" (Scarry, 1999) or on the "right to beauty" (McCormick, 2010;

Clammer, 2019; Cabiddu, 2021). See also Elbaz and Alfasi (2023). An interesting study by Kaplan and Kaplan (1982) provides a framework in which to interpret the beauty of the "urbanscape". See finally Heath (1988).

15 For example, in commenting on an article on the (spontaneous) beauty of cities (Cozzolino, 2021), Araabi (2022) points out that beauty is for the large part an upper-class and conservative concern. This point has emerged several times and from different voices during seminars and conferences.

16 To avoid misunderstandings, it is necessary to emphasise that these observations concern the city as a whole, especially in dense urban situations. Overall, a city is not a work of art. However, in cities there are certain urban structures and objects that can possess the characteristics of a work of art (they have been intentionally conceived and designed to express specific aesthetic meanings). This is the case of many monumental structures, such as certain spaces for collective use (for example, squares, stations, large places of worship). On this see Romano (2008 and 2010).

17 For a long time, Alexander pursued a similar line of reasoning, attempting to connect the significance of complexity to visual appreciation. He is renowned for developing the idea of "living structure" in order to elucidate how architectural variety and details contribute to the experience of beauty. In essence, his concept underscores the capacity of the built environment to be visually dynamic and alive – regardless of the fact that the architectural complexity under consideration organically evolved over time or was intentionally designed. Recent studies have developed this discourse mathematically, trying to make Alexander's intuition more objective (e.g. Jiang, 2019 and de Rijke et al. 2020). However, while the concept of living structure embraces complexity thinking, one must acknowledge that it is limited to visual and material aspects. The challenge is finding a way to extend the understanding of urban beauty to include other aspects (e.g. social and behavioural aspects) and thus better represent the entire urban experience.

18 *Venice Syndrome*, a reportage by François Prost deals with this issue (http://francoisprost.com/portfolio-item/venice-syndrome/ accessed August 2023).

19 On the concept of *genius loci*, see especially Norberg-Schulz (1979). Interesting reflections can also be found in Bacchini and Piras (2021).

20 An interesting work on this topic is Boeing (2018).

21 Several authors dealing with aesthetics have used Naples as a remarkable example of this kind of experience. Walter Benjamin (1925) described the city as an endless sequence of surprises within a highly complex and porous built environment. He depicted the city as a stage of popular improvisation and representation: "Buildings are […] all divided into innumerable, simultaneously animated theatres. Balcony, courtyard, window, gateway, staircase, roof are at the same time stage and boxes. Even the most wretched pauper is sovereign in the dim, dual awareness of participating, in all his destitution, in one of the pictures of Neapolitan street life" (Benjamin, 1925/1978: 167). In a similar vein, in his famous *Italian Journey 1786–1788*, Johann Wolfgang von Goethe wrote: "I won't say another word about the beauties of the city and its situation, which

have been described and praised so often [...]". And he continues: "Naples is a paradise; everyone lives in a state of intoxicated self-forgetfulness, myself included" (Goethe, 1817/1982: 198).

22 Well-known reflections on the positive role of complexity are provided also by Sennett (1970).

23 An interesting study on this subject is Portugali (2011).

24 See, for example, Van Geert and Wagemans (2020: 135).

25 See, for example, Chipman (1977: 269) and Krpan and van Tilburg (2022: 4): "The most beautiful images are the ones that are both complex and characterised by order". An interesting work regarding complexity and architecture is Brielmann et al. (2022). On the specific issue of urban complexity, see Salingaros (2018).

26 Similarly, Moore (1942: 42) writes: "Variety without unity is confusing, and unity without variety is monotonous and uninteresting".

27 On this issue, see also Nasar (1994) and Post et al. (2016). Although mainly dealing with architecture, other interesting works in this regard are Mehaffy (2020), Salingaros (2020), and Mehaffy and Salingaros (2018).

28 A valuable attempt to provide practical and theoretical suggestions on how to generate beauty at a large scale is Porta et al. (2016). Other interesting reflections are in Mehaffy (2008), Mehaffy and Salingaros (2017) and Porqueddu (2018).

References

Akkerman, A. (2000). Harmonies of urban design and discords of city-form: Urban aesthetics in the rise of western civilisation. *Journal of Urban Design*, 5 (3): 267–290.

Alexander, C. (1979). *The Timeless Way of Building*, vol. 1. New York: Oxford University Press.

Alexander, C. (1980). *The Nature of Order: The Process of Creating Life.* London: Routledge, 2002.

Alexander, C. (2021). New concepts in complexity theory arising from studies in the field of architecture: An overview of the four books of the nature of order with emphasis on the scientific problems which are raised. In J. Portugali (ed.), *Handbook on Cities and Complexity.* Cheltenham: Edward Elgar, 210–232.

Araabi, H.F. (2022). Commentary: beauty in urban design-oppression or emancipation? *Urban Design International.* doi:10.1057/s41289-022-00202-z.

Armstrong, T., Detweiler-Bedell, B. (2008). Beauty as an emotion: The exhilarating prospect of mastering a challenging world. *Review of General Psychology*, 12 (4):305–329.

Arnheim, R. (1966). Order and complexity in landscape design. In R. Arnheim (ed.), *Toward a Psychology of Art*. Berkeley and Los Angeles, CA: University of California Press, 123–135.

Bacchini, F., Piras, N. (2021). Can a city be relocated? Exploring the metaphysics of context-dependency. *Argumenta*, 7 (1): 217–231.

Benjamin, W. (1925, 19 August). Neapel. *Frankfurter Zeitung*. English translation: Naples. In P. Demetz (ed.), *Reflections: Essays, Aphorisms, Autobiographical Writings*. New York: Houghton Mifflin Harcourt, 1978, 163–173.

Biddulph, M. (2012). The problem with thinking about or for urban design. *Journal of Urban Design*, 17 (1): 1–20.

Bodei, R. (1995). *Le forme del bello*. Bologna: il Mulino.

Boeing, G. (2018). Measuring the complexity of urban form and design. *Urban Design International*, 23 (4): 281–292.

Brielmann, A.A., Buras, N.H., Salingaros, N.A., Taylor, R.P. (2022). What happens in your brain when you walk down the street? Implications of architectural proportions, biophilia, and fractal geometry for urban science. *Urban Science*, 6 (1): 1–35.

Carr, O. (2022). A legal challenge to “beauty” in the National Planning Policy Framework 2021. *Planning Theory & Practice*, 23 (4): 604–607.

Cabiddu, M.A. (2021). *Bellezza. Per un sistema nazionale*. Napoli: Doppiavoce.

Cecchetti, M., Baker, S. (2011). For sensitive skin: On the transformation of architecture into design. *Annali d'italianistica*, 29: 237–252.

Chiodo, S. (2017). Ideality of beauty. *Materiali di Estetica*, 4 (1): 96–114.

Chiodo, S. (2019). Judging the value of beauty: From aesthetics to ethics. *Valori e Valutazioni*, 23: 31–36.

Chipman, S.F. (1977). Complexity and structure in visual patterns. *Journal of Experimental Psychology: General*, 106 (3): 269–301.

Clammer, J. (2019). *Cultural Rights and Justice. Sustainable Development, the Arts and the Body*. Singapore: Palgrave Macmillan.

Cozzolino, S. (2021). On the spontaneous beauty of cities: Neither design nor chaos. *Urban Design International*, 27: 43–52.

Cozzolino, S., Polívka, J., Fox-Kämper, R., Reimer, M., Kummel, O. (2020). What is urban design? A proposal for a common understanding. *Journal of Urban Design*, 25 (1): 35–49.

De Franco, A., Moroni, S. (2023). The city as an information system: Urban agency, experiential inputs and planning measures. *Cities*, 134: 1–8.

de Rijke, C. A., Macassa, G., Sandberg, M., Jiang, B. (2020). Living structure as an empirical measurement of city morphology. *ISPRS International Journal of Geo-Information*, 9 (11): 1–16.

Eco, U. (2004). *Storia della bellezza*. Milano: Bompiani.

Elbaz, A., Alfasi, N. (2023). What about beauty in planning theory and practice? *Journal of Planning Literature* (Online ahead of print).

Goethe, J.W. (1817). *Italienische Reise*. English translation: *Italian Journey 1786–1788*. San Francisco: North Point Press, 1982.

Heath, T. (1988). Behavioral and perceptual aspects of the aesthetics of urban environments. In J. Nasar (ed.), *Environmental Aesthetics: Theory, Research, and Application*. Cambridge: Cambridge University Press, 6–10.

Hillman, J. (2018). *City & Soul*. Thompson, CT: Spring Publications.

Hoch, C. (2006). Emotions and planning. *Planning Theory & Practice*, 7 (4): 367–382.

Jacobs, J. (1961). *The Death and Life of Great American Cities*. New York: Random House.

Jiang, B. (2019). Living structure down to earth and up to heaven: Christopher Alexander. *Urban Science*, 3 (3): 1–20.

Jorgensen, A. (2011). Beyond the view: Future directions in landscape aesthetics research. *Landscape and Urban Planning*, 100 (4): 353–355.

Kaplan, S., Kaplan, R. (1982). *Cognition and Environment: Coping in an Uncertain World*. New York: Praeger.

Krpan, D., van Tilburg, W.A.P. (2022). The aesthetic quality model: Complexity and randomness as foundations of visual beauty by signaling quality. *Psychology of Aesthetics, Creativity, and the Arts* (forthcoming).

Lang, J. (2006). *Urban Design*. London: Routledge.

Le Corbusier (1923). Vers une architecture. Paris: Crès et Cie. English translation: *Toward a New Architecture*. New York: Dover, 1986.

Lynch, K. (1981). *A Theory of Good City Form*. Cambridge, MA: The MIT Press.

McCormick, P.T. (2010). A right to beauty: A fair share of milk and honey for the poor. *Theological Studies*, 71 (3): 702–720.

McGreevy, M.P. (2017). Complexity as the telos of postmodern planning and design: Designing better cities from the bottom-up. *Planning Theory*, 17 (3): 355–374.

Mehaffy, M.W. (2008). Generative methods in urban design: a progress assessment. *Journal of Urbanism*, 1 (1): 57–75.

Mehaffy, M.W. (2020). The Impacts of symmetry in architecture and urbanism: Toward a new research agenda. *Buildings*, 10 (12): 1–20.

Mehaffy, M.W, Salingaros, N.A. (2017). *Design for a Living Planet: Settlement, Science, & the Human Future*. Portland, OR: Sustasis Press.

Mehaffy, M.W., Salingaros, N.A. (2018, 19 February). The neuroscience of architecture: The good, the bad, and the beautiful. *Traditional Building Magazine*.

Moroni, S. (2019). Critically reconsidering orthodox ideas: Planning as teleocratic intervention and planning as a rational decision method. *Planning Theory & Practice*, 20 (3): 323–338.

Moore, J.S. (1942). Beauty as harmony. *The Journal of Aesthetics and Art Criticism*, 2 (7): 40–42.

Nasar, J. (1994). Urban design aesthetics: The evaluative qualities of building exteriors. *Environment and Behavior*, 26 (3): 377–401.

Nasar, J. (ed.) (1988). *Environmental Aesthetics: Theory, Research and Applications*. Cambridge: Cambridge University Press.

Norberg-Schulz, C. (1979). *Genius Loci: Towards a Phenomenology of Architecture*. New York: Rizzoli.

Noyes, C.E. (1907). *The Gate of Appreciation: Studies in the Relation of Art to Life*. Boston, MA: Houghton Mifflin.

Palermo, P.C., Ponzini, D. (2012). At the crossroads between urban planning and urban design: Critical lessons from three Italian case studies. *Planning Theory & Practice*, 13 (3): 445–460.

Ponzini, D. (2011). Large scale development projects and star architecture in the absence of democratic politics: The case of Abu Dhabi, UAE. *Cities*, 28 (3): 251–259.

Porqueddu, E. (2018). Toward the open city: Design and research for emergent urban systems. *Urban Design International*, 23: 236–248.

Porta, S., Rofé, Y., Vidoli, M. (2016). The city and the grid: Building beauty at large scale. In M. Mehaffy (ed.), *A City Is Not a Tree. 50th Anniversary Edition*. Portland, OR: Sustasis Press, 163–184.

Portugali, J. (2011). *Complexity, Cognition and the City*. Berlin: Springer.

Post, R.A.G., Blijlevens, J., Hekkert, P. (2016). "To preserve unity while almost allowing for chaos": Testing the aesthetic principle of unity-in-variety in product design. *Acta Psychologica*, 163: 142–152.

Rofè, Y., Porta, S., Ingham, S., Andrews, C.R., Ettlinger, O., Robazza, P., Alexander, M.M. (2020). Building beauty: A new program teaching students to help heal the world. In A. Sayigh (ed.), *Green Buildings and Renewable Energy*. Cham: Springer, 611–622.

Rogers, E.N. (1946). Ricostruzione: dall'oggetto d'uso alla città. *Domus*, 215: 2–5.

Romano, M. (2008). *La città come opera d'arte*. Torino: Einauidi.

Romano, M. (2010). *Ascesa e declino della città europea*. Milano: Cortina.

Ryser, J. (2022). Is beauty in the eye of the beholder? *Planning Theory & Practice*, 23 (4): 621–626.

Saito, Y. (2007). *Everyday Aesthetics*. Oxford: Oxford University Press.

Salingaros, N.A. (2018). Adaptive versus random complexity. *New Design Ideas*, 2 (2): 51–61.

Salingaros, N.A. (2020). Symmetry gives meaning to architecture. *Symmetry: Culture and Science*, 31 (3), 231–260.

Scarry, E. (1999). *On Beauty and Being Just*. Princeton, NJ: Princeton University Press.

Scruton, R. (2007). In search of the aesthetic. *The British Journal of Aesthetics*, 47 (3): 232–250.

Scruton, R. (2021). *The Aesthetics of Architecture*. Princeton, NJ: Princeton University Press.

Sennett, R. (1970). *The Uses of Disorder: Personal Identity and City Life*. New York: Verso Books, 2021.

Shiner, L. (2003). *The Invention of Art: A Cultural History*. Chicago, IL: University of Chicago Press.

Skov, M., Nadal, M. (2021). The nature of beauty: Behavior, cognition, and neurobiology. *Annals of the New York Academy of Sciences*, 1488 (1): 44–55.

Slaev, A.D., Cozzolino, S., Nozharova, B., Ilieva, J. (2022). The spontaneous rules of spontaneous development. *Environment and Planning B*, 49 (9): 2392–2408.

Sitte, C. (1889). *Der Städtebau nach seinen Künstlerischen Grundsätzen*. English translation: *The Art of Building Cities: City Building According to its Artistic Fundamentals*. Ravenio, 1979.

Sternberg, E. (2000). An integrative theory of urban design. *Journal of the American Planning Association*, 66 (3): 265–278.

Stolnitz, J. (1961). Beauty: Some stages in the history of an idea. *Journal of the History of Ideas*, 22 (2): 185–204.

Swyngedouw, E., Moulaert, F., Rodriguez, A. (2002). Neoliberal urbanisation in Europe: Large–scale urban development projects and the new urban policy. *Antipode* 34 (3): 542–577.

Talen, E., Ellis, C. (2002). Beyond relativism: Reclaiming the search for good city form. *Journal of Planning Education and Research*, 22 (1): 36–49.

Taylor, N. (1999). Anglo-American town planning theory since 1945: Three significant developments but no paradigm shifts. *Planning Perspectives* 14 (4): 327–345.

Taylor, N. (2009). Legibility and aesthetics in urban design. *Journal of Urban Design*, 14 (2): 189–202.

Tursić, M. (2019). The city as an aesthetic space. *City*, 23 (2): 205–221.

Van Geert, E., Wagemans, J. (2020). Order, complexity, and aesthetic appreciation. *Psychology of Aesthetics, Creativity, and the Arts*, 14: 135–154.

Vercellone, F. (2008). *Oltre la bellezza*. Bologna: Il Mulino.

Wilson, W.H. (1994). *The City Beautiful Movement*. Baltimore, MD: Johns Hopkins University Press.

Wright, F.L. (1935). Broadacre City: A new community plan. In R.T. LeGates, F. Staut (eds), *The City Reader*. London and New York: Routledge, 2011, 345–350.

7 Conclusion

Accepting the challenge in planning theory and practice

1 Introduction

Urban complexity, as a result of the presence of multiple action and continuous interaction, challenges planners as they are inevitably forced to deal with problems of limited understanding of truly *dynamic* processes and structural ignorance of *open* future events. In practice, this means not only that the chances for planners to guide urban development towards predetermined, specific outcomes are inevitably limited, but also that complexity itself is something that must be preserved, and not intrinsically counteracted or avoided. In other words, the main responsibility of planning should be to favour the development of cities that are congenial places for (positive aspects of) complexity to flourish.

2 Focus: Limits and potential of planning

2.1 Range of possible actions

A city, or an urban neighbourhood, can be described as more or less adaptable by considering the *range of possible actions* that can potentially readdress its development. This expression refers to the overall space that urban agents have to adapt and change their current state of affairs. This "action space" can be identified by analysing the type and intensity of actions that can be undertaken by urban agents in a particular area, and which therefore eventually contribute to its adaptive evolution.[1]

Note that this view expresses the *potential* of a system to host and accommodate a multiplicity of (unpredictable) actions. But it says nothing about its actual future appearance. It expresses an urban area's general propensity and predisposition to rely on future

DOI: 10.4324/9781003454304-7

spontaneous developments deriving from multiple actions. Terms like "propensity" and "predisposition" are used to underscore that urban agents can use this action space to a greater or lesser extent. This eventuality depends on urban agents' plans, opportunities, needs, means, desires, and aspirations to change and adapt their environment. Therefore, this is a *space of possibilities.*

In short, a city (or parts of it) that guarantees space for a great variety of actions is more likely to generate self-adaptive dynamics. Conversely, a city with a limited amount of action space will eventually develop and generate steadier configurations less open to self-adaptive processes of change.

In conclusion, not all social-spatial systems exhibit the same degree of spontaneity and self-adaptability. This difference depends on the variety and intensity of actions that can potentially reshape their future dynamics.

To avoid misunderstandings, it is important to anticipate an issue that will be discussed at length in Section 3 of this chapter: the "space of action" is not necessarily broader in a situation of unqualified "*license*" but it is so, instead, in a situation of "*freedom* under the law" (provided that the law is understood in an appropriate manner) (Leoni, 1961).[2]

2.2 Action and conditions of action

Given the foregoing discussion, in what follows we shall reflect on three main points in relation to public planning; that is, planning deliberately done by a public authority (e.g. local government) with certain exclusive and legitimate prerogatives.

2.2.1 First point: On what does planning act? What is the object of planning?

Firstly, public planning may intervene directly only on the *conditions* (of action) and not on the *actions* of individuals. It can only manipulate the conditions in which actions are carried out, but without being able – even more so in a constitutional democracy – to intervene directly and materially on the actions; for example, by forcing some individuals to move each weekend to do their shopping and find entertainment in certain new regenerated neighbourhoods, or to build their dwelling by themselves.

Note that the impossibility of directly channelling all actions entails the impossibility of determining – and preserving over time – specific physical-spatial configurations or specific distributions of goods. As Alain Bertaud (2018: 24) writes on cities' dynamics: "Over the mid and long term they are largely unpredictable, and it is futile to pretend they are the result of careful planning". Compare with Jane Jacobs (1958: 127): "There is no logic that can be superimposed on the city; people make it". But technocratic planning (employing comprehensive and detailed functional zoning plans) tries instead to do precisely this: to design the comprehensive desired end state and impose it – superimpose it – on behavioural dynamics; in this case, the intent is to have the rules and the spatial configurations coincide. Also certain forms of engineeristic transport planning seek to impose specific patterns of behaviour rather than background conditions for mobility. In both cases, this has resulted in ineffective and inefficient results, which planners tend to attribute to actors – considered myopic and resistant to "optimal" plans – rather than to the velleity of their tools.

Another interesting aspect is that the particular distinction drawn between *conditions* and *actions* makes it clear that there is not necessarily isomorphism between them. This can be explained with an example concerning the much-discussed topic of *creative cities*. According to many, "a necessary component of a creative city are governance systems that are creative, imaginative, flexible and accommodating" (Smith and Warfield, 2008: 287). But it is the city – that is, its citizens – who must actually be creative, not the urban policies in themselves. It is not the policy-maker's job to be creative; it is the task of ordinary citizens and entrepreneurs. Policy-makers must grant the conditions – not necessarily innovative and creative – so that the actions of individuals and groups in civil society can be creative (Moroni, 2011; Cozzolino, 2019). For instance, the local government does not always need to do something "positive" in order to have a creative city. It must more often simply refrain from doing too much, and grant instead stable and credible simple rules. As Gert-Jan Hospers (2003a: 149) notes, it is an illusion to believe that we can force urban creativity directly: "The unpredictability surrounding creativity and innovation means that a tailor-made, unambiguous creative competitive strategy for urban environment is not available". In other words: "Creative cities cannot be constructed from the ground up […]. In their enthusiasm, local authorities sometimes tend to forget this" (Hospers, 2003b: 266).

2.2.2 Second point: What is the domain of planning?

Secondly, public planning may, in actual fact, control only *some* of the conditions actually relevant to the action of individuals. The main fields in which public planning may intervene directly are, ultimately, those of (*intentionally created) material conditions* – and that may occur for instance by providing public infrastructures and public spaces – and of (*intentionally created) immaterial conditions* – especially by means of rules and standards. A substantial portion of the conditions of actions (e.g. conditions *unintentionally* produced, like emerging spatial and social patterns: Chapters 2 and 3) will always elude both planners' predictive capacity and their direct control. This suggests that planners should be humbler (Moroni, 2010b; Moroni and Chiffi, 2022). Indeed, the social world is partially opaque to them due to unintentional effects, spontaneous self-coordinating phenomena, tacit (and therefore inaccessible) forms of dispersed knowledge. To conclude: "One of the tenets of complexity science is that you have little control of emergent patterns" (Lewin, 1993: 218).

2.2.3 Third point: How can planning intervene?

The third significant point is this: not only is public planning only capable of effectively intervening on *some conditions*, but, if we recognise the complex and multi-layered nature of social-spatial systems, it is only capable of doing so in *certain ways*: both because the complexity of the system makes it impossible to intervene in other ways, and because there are positive aspects in preserving complexity itself.

For instance, considering for illustrative purposes only the public rule-framework, it seems necessary to abandon a strictly *instrumental* view of law and rules.[3] In an instrumental perspective, law is understood primarily as a tool or means to achieve desired concrete goals; it can be shaped in any way necessary to fulfil our purposes. The identification of ends is considered to be totally open and without limits of any sort (Tamanaha, 2006). This idea of law was clearly influenced by the Enlightenment thinkers' illusion regarding the power of human reason: "The Enlightenment confidence that humans can shape […] the conditions of their existence encouraged the instrumental view of law" (Tamanaha, 2006: 23). By contrast, the law must be interpreted (not as an instrument for achieving some sort of specific outcome, but rather) as an abstract meta-framework for the peaceful co-existence of many different actors with incommensurable and continuously changing goals.

3 Discussion: A renewed planning approach

In the following sections (and on the basis of the distinction between private and public spaces[4]) we explore the three main ways in which planning can intervene in cities by taking the complexity deriving from multiple actions and interactions seriously into account. It can do so: (i) by setting appropriate rules to regulate private spaces and buildings; (ii) by favouring and safeguarding the several property (of private spaces); (iii) by providing adequate public spaces and infrastructure.

It should be stressed that we consider these to be the three main spheres of local planning intervention; they do not represent the entirety of desirable urban policies but only those more strictly connected with planning issues.[5]

The following discussion derives mainly from the assumption that complexity is an *empirical* phenomenon: that is, recognition of the existence and particular ways in which certain kinds of phenomena arise and function. Obviously, some *values* are also implicated here; but these are minimum values, such as the right of each individual to choose his/her own life-plan, the right of each individual to a sphere protected from intrusion/damage by others, the right of everyone to free association with others, and so on.

3.1 First element: Framework rules (for private spaces)

The private part of the city should be considered as the dynamic result of an order emerging organically from the bottom up. From this perspective, planners should not design or regulate the city as if they were able to grasp all of people's various preferences and desires in advance. Instead they should provide rules and standards that allow complexity and multiple lifestyles to flourish. Recognition of the variety of user interests and the unpredictability of future types of use is therefore essential. What we need are rules that grant mutually reinforcing sets of expectations; these rules have to be rigid enough so as to support our expectations, but open enough to allow for emerging situations and creative human responses (Boettke, 1990: 76). Observe that, from this perspective, *systems of rules* and *social-spatial patterns* do not coincide: the former are – if appropriately set – the precondition for the emergence of the latter.

As previously pointed out and as regards rules set by the public authority (e.g. the local government), we should first of all reject, in planning as in other fields, what we called the strictly "instrumental" idea of law. The law (i.e. rules, regulations, standards) does not serve – and cannot serve in complex, dynamic systems – to obtain specific results, for example a particular urban configuration; rather, it serves to allow peaceful coexistence, especially in those places such as cities where multiple actions for different purposes are concentrated.

In this regard, it is possible to specify four fundamental formal characteristics that the rules of use of land and buildings should have.

Firstly, we should prefer *relational rules*, which are abstract and general, rather than *directional rules*, which are specific and particular. Relational rules do not concern concrete overall physical outcomes, but the general process of action and interaction. They refer to standard situations or actions, not to specific ones, and apply equally to everyone, or, at least, to broad classes or categories of people, and not to specific individuals/groups or tracts of land. They reconcile the actions of individuals solely in relation to their "typical features" (i.e. their repeatable, time-independent, and situation-independent aspects, such as building and transforming objects in space which have volume/extension and interact with other objects), but not in relation to their "specific features" (i.e. their unrepeatable, time-dependent and situation-dependent aspects, such as constructing or transforming building A, in neighbourhood B, at time C) (O'Driscoll and Rizzo, 1985). Therefore, relational rules are not focused on predetermined forms and patterns but on the stepwise process by which ordered spatial configurations autonomously emerge from actions and interactions.[6] Introducing general and abstract rules that refer only to typical actions entails recognising the importance and desirability of the creative and unpredictable multiplicity of urban actions. By contrast, insisting on specific and particular rules entails selecting the paths of action *a priori* (disregarding the autonomous and creative role of each single action). To conclude: relational, abstract and general, rules allow individuals – citizens, developers, architects, designers, etc. – to respond to new situations through innovative action prompted by their unique knowledge of the circumstances of time and place, and their means.

Secondly, we should prefer *simple* rules to complicated ones. The appropriate response to more and more complex social-spatial systems should actually be a greater reliance on simple rules (Webster and Lai, 2003). Simple rules are rules that: (i) are understandable and determinate (that is, written in a clear language that does not generate unnecessary uncertainty); (ii) imply a binary response (responses to simple rules are essentially dichotomous in nature: one either complies or does not comply with those rules; in other words, there is a clear-cut, binary yes/no answer); (iii) avoid introducing a high number of complicated distinctions; (iv) are part of regulative sets that have a low number of rules and a low rule density (Moroni et al., 2018). Not only simple rules are more likely to be enforced than complex rules, diminish administrative costs (i.e. all the costs necessary to run a certain legal system correctly), and reduce the risk of unscrupulous public officers taking advantage of the elbow room afforded by a fuzzy legal framework; but above all they are better suited to solving interaction problems among persons with different ideas of the good and lifestyles, and increase the capacity of the social-spatial system to take advantage of dispersed knowledge (i.e., the diffused contextual know-how that emerges and develops in a dynamic and continuous way).[7]

Thirdly, we should favour *negative* rules over *positive* rules: that is, proscriptive rules over prescriptive rules. In other words, we should prefer rules telling us what *must not be done*: for instance, which negative externalities we must avoid producing when using or transforming urban spaces, as opposed to what *must be done* in positive terms. The externalities we have to deal with are not those presumed to impinge upon social efficiency, as in orthodox welfare economics, but those that infringe upon what we consider legitimate individual rights or titles. The point here is not, therefore, "market failures", but the institutional constraints required to minimise interpersonal conflict (Cordato, 2004). Note that positive rules tend to select the *results* of urban actions and make them mandatory, while negative rules only define the *boundaries* of possible actions; that is, the spheres within which urban actors can freely operate, interact and negotiate. In this perspective, it is possible to control not so much the *uses* of private buildings and private spaces as the undesired *effects* of such uses, regardless of what they might be.[8] Formulating primarily negative rules fosters the openness of cities to unforeseen developments, while safeguarding important rights. Whilst in the case of positive rules, individuals' actions are coordinated in their details by a visible hand according to some end-state plan, in the case of negative rules individuals' actions are self-coordinated once certain harms are prohibited (Kasper and Streit, 1998: 97).[9]

Fourthly, we should favour *stable* rules; that is, rules that can only be changed through strictly pre-defined and non-discretional procedures, and thanks to forms of super-majorities. In other words, a simple majority is not enough in this case, and a qualified majority is instead required. Stable rules are decisive, since ordinary citizens, landowners, entrepreneurs, developers and so forth, need to clearly know the "rules of the game", not merely for their short-term actions, but also for their long-term endeavours.

Rules of this kind (that is, relational, simple, negative and stable rules: see Table 7.1) are typical of what have been called *urban codes* (Moroni, 2015, 2023; Alfasi, 2018). These rules serve to reduce, though not to eliminate, uncertainty. They narrow the range of possible urban actions to some typical and general classes. They are end-independent in the sense that they leave urban actors free to choose their own ends and act accordingly, provided that they do not cause direct and tangible harm to other actors while fulfilling them.[10]

Urban codes are therefore not *patterning-instruments* (such as orthodox zoning plans), but *framework-instruments*; that is, they are not shaping-devices but filter-devices (Moroni, 2015). In this sense, they can enable a *pattern-coordination* among multiple agents (not a *coordination of details*; see Figure 7.1).[11] As Nurit Alfasi (2018: 386) writes,

> codes and abstract principles make it possible to evade the problematic of creating overly specific regulations, imposing end-solutions and issuing orders to the numerous urban actors about what to build [...]. In fact, coding is acknowledged as the necessary backdrop for the functioning of the built environment as a complex, adaptive system.

Table 7.1 Types of rules: urban codes vs. orthodox land-use plans

Types of rules	
Urban codes	*Orthodox land-use plans*
Relational	Directional
Intrinsically simple	Generally complicated
Mainly proscriptive	Mainly prescriptive
Stable (not modifiable with ordinary procedures)	Typically unstable (frequently revised)

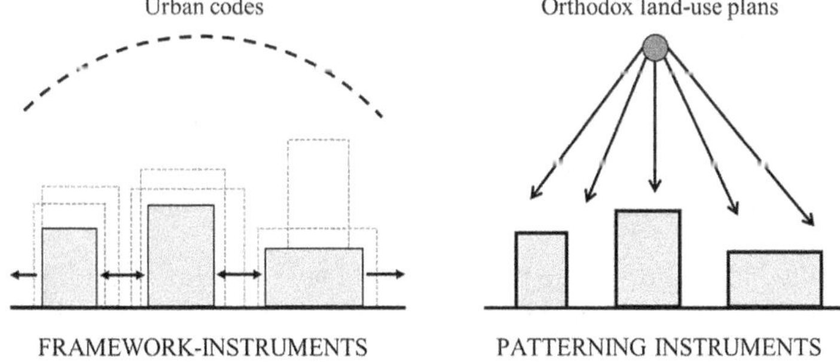

Figure 7.1 Framework-instruments vs. patterning-instruments. Diagram derived from Hakim, 2008

3.2 Second element: Several property (of private spaces)

An urban environment open to dynamic processes is one in which, in regard to property, there is (i) *variety* and (ii) *polycentrism.*

By "variety", we mean a situation in which many various ownership arrangements and organisational forms in regard to land and buildings are in place and/or can be invented (Andersson and Moroni, 2014).

By "polycentrism", we mean a situation in which the decision-making power regarding (private) urban objects is distributed among many independent owners. The more independent owners – single or group – there are in the urban realm, the more this power is diffused. This is the situation that Friedrich von Hayek (1960, 1982 and 1988) calls "several property".[12] As he writes,

> individual decision presupposed individual spheres of control, and thus became possible only with the evolution of several property, whose development, in turn, laid the foundation for the growth of an extended order transcending the perception of the headman or chief – or of the collectivity.
>
> (Hayek, 1988: 50)

Several property is therefore a situation of *decentralised jurisdiction*; that is, a situation that recognises the "bounded jurisdiction" of individuals and groups over physical resources "so as to permit them the freedom to act on the basis of their own personal and local knowledge. This enables individuals and associations to harness the knowledge in their possession" (Barnett, 1998: 63). In short, the expression *several property* "makes it clearer that jurisdiction to use resources is dispersed among the 'several' – meaning 'diverse, many, numerous, distinct, particular, or separate' – persons and associations that comprise a society, rather than being reposed in a monolithic centralised institution" (Barnett, 1998: 65).[13] Observe how, from this point of view, it is even possible to advance new arguments against monopoly situations (in cases of scarce resources such as land).

Both elements, *variety* and *polycentrism*, can be favoured by public policies.

On the one hand, public policies should give individuals and groups as much room as possible to *experiment* and *invent* new forms of property arrangements and specific organisational forms. This is possible by not rigidly straitjacketing in advance the array of possible solutions (Brunetta and Moroni, 2012).[14]

On the other hand, public policies may favour *access* to ownership and a more widespread *distribution* of ownership of urban assets (e.g. houses, shops, businesses) by, for instance,[15] (i) avoiding any restriction on access to residential ownership (e.g. those defining who can be owners and who can be resident in the property: Hamill, 2022); (ii) implementing particular fiscal policies to favour access to – and diffusion of – any kind of property (e.g. incentives and tax exemptions for access to the housing market, particularly in the case of first-time-buyers: Lind, 2007; mechanisms to promote small-businesses and micro-enterprise developments in cities: Jones, 2007);[16] and (iii) enacting adequate informative policies (e.g. new digital platforms that increase knowledge options and general transparency in regard, for instance, to financial possibilities, requisite licences and permits, market opportunities).

From this perspective, public policies must discourage an excessive concentration of real-estate ownership in one individual's hands. This does not necessarily mean that public policies have to "fight" against large urban agents in themselves. Instead, they should create conditions in which small, less powerful agents can also participate in the system.

3.3 Third element: Adequate public spaces and infrastructures

In this case, what public planning can do is to produce collectively significant public spaces and infrastructure, without overlooking the complex nature of social-spatial systems and the active and creative role of actions (Cozzolino et al., 2020). Public spaces and infrastructure not only grant certain levels of equity; they also work as supporting structures for the evolution of cities without the need to control in detail every single action: in other words, these elements guarantee one of the necessary conditions for self-coordinated social-spatial systems to emerge (Holcombe, 2012; Andersson and Andersson, 2017). In this perspective, upfront planning measures and design are welcome. Firstly we shall consider (i) the issue of *public spaces*, followed by (ii) the issue of *public infrastructure.*

3.3.1 Public spaces

As regards open public spaces (e.g. plazas, squares, parks), the first issue can be stated as follows. Liveable open public spaces are continuously used by people for different reasons, at different times; however, public spaces must be designed and created only *where* and *when* relevant, avoiding dullness and waste. In fact, above a certain threshold, public spaces may stop being beneficial and turn into the same safety problem as "streets without eyes" (Jacobs, 1961). In other words, an unnecessary abundance of public spaces may generate a problem of control, moving from spontaneous and bottom-up control to "police control" (Habraken, 1998: 158), as well as raising significant problems of maintenance and public expenditure. Contrary to what is often assumed in today's debates, public spaces should not be "venerated" but instead questioned for their concrete utility in light of multiple urban actions and interactions.[17]

Secondly, certain public spaces, such as squares, parks or pedestrian areas, must be physically designed to host a plurality of possible actions and activities, and exhibit a high degree of internal adaptability over time. In other words, their design and physical conformation must not be such as to permit only a scant number of possible uses and activities, but must instead be capable of accommodating change (Roggema, 2014; Bergevoet and van Tuijl, 2016). More precisely, the desirable qualities of these (public) spaces are: (i) *looseness*, that is, the capacity to include simultaneously a variety of different activities (Franck and Stevens, 2006); (ii) *robustness*, that is, the ability to accommodate new uses without significant change to their physical form (Carmona et al., 2010); and (iii) *polyvalence*, that is the ability to accept multiple reinterpretations according to the evolving users' perspectives (Hertzberger, 1991). To conclude, when possible, designers and planners should avoid imposing detailed and rigidly determined meanings or functions on public space; instead, they should try to create flexible environments in which multiple meanings and functions can emerge from the everyday actions of users. The need to have flexible public spaces stems from the certainty that these cannot be designed in such a way that all contingent problems or needs can be solved *once-and-forever*. From a design perspective, this means providing "open" solutions to unpredictable problems. In this sense, a practical approach to a situation that is subject to change is a design that embraces *changefulness* as a permanent factor (Hertzberger, 1991).

Thirdly, it is important that also the *interface* between public and private spaces is adaptable and flexible. The public space should therefore not be conceived as impenetrable and "closed in upon itself" (sufficient unto itself), but as porous and "welcoming" to changes of private activities and businesses at street level: for example, the opening of a new restaurant which installs tables and chairs outside, the transformation of an open private space (e.g. a garden) into a showroom window, the opening of a small street food stall in front of a wall, the creation of pedestrian access to a space that was previously residential and now used as a store. In short, public spaces must be conceived and designed, from the outset, as able to accommodate set-back adaptations, changes in transparency, changes in accesses (created or blocked) of private counterparts and so on.[18]

3.3.2 Public infrastructures

Turning to the issue of infrastructure, various factors need to be considered if complexity emerging from actions and interactions is to be taken fully into account.

First of all and from a very general point of view, before building new infrastructure, it is essential to consider two options seriously: (i) do nothing[19] and (ii) make the use of existing infrastructure more efficient. In both instances, these options should not be viewed as alternatives in the purely logical sense, but as concrete and potentially beneficial options (Priemus, 2007, 2010 and 2012). Some sections of high-speed railway, in Italy for example, have been designed and constructed without seriously considering the much less costly and, in some cases, more effective alternative to modernise the existing routes (Ponti, 2007 and 2015).

Secondly, we can no longer remain indifferent to citizens' and consumers' purposes, for instance in the case of transport infrastructure (as has been typically the case with orthodox, uncritical, top-down planning approaches). Consider the problematic case of the automobile. The usual approach of the technocratic planner is to consider car drivers as short-sighted passive users (and, therefore, to be re-educated and redirected); without in the least considering that they are instead *active agents* for whom the car enters their plans in various and differentiated ways. Approaches indifferent to the theme of the action have suggested that it is easy to change a behaviour – e.g. that of motorists – considered imitative and obtuse. Decades of policies based on the "modal shift" hypothesis, for example, have by contrast shown that it is not easy to switch significant amounts of mobility from private vehicles to the various forms of collective transport (in particular, those on rails) (Ponti, 2007; Ponti et al., 2013). In fact, people use cars not only because of the habits they have grown accustomed to but also because, quite frequently, no other mode of transportation can fully substitute for the convenience and abilities that a car provides in certain situations. This, of course, does not imply that we should refrain from investing in railways or other forms of collective transportation, or that we should avoid addressing congestion issues resulting from car usage; it means that we should do so by taking seriously the fact that we are dealing with *active agents* to whom we can – and must – provide alternatives (that is, various options), but who we cannot re-direct *en masse* where we prefer. Infrastructures should therefore be understood more as "opportunities" (offered to complex systems whose self-coordinating nature cannot be compressed) than as "levers".

Thirdly, if new infrastructure is contemplated, small-scale interventions should be accorded preference over large-scale interventions.[20] Given the small-scale and process-oriented nature of these interventions, they cannot offer a comprehensive vision of the future. Rather, they become part of a process which is never meant to be completed but open and incremental (Porqueddu, 2018). There are several reasons for this approach. In a complex world, large infrastructure projects are more subject to cost estimation errors;[21] they entail greater financial and technical risks and are subject to long, often uncontrollable execution times; and they are inevitably far less adaptable to the areas through which they pass, and hardly exploit existing network economies at all. In contrast, small-scale infrastructure projects are less subject to forecasting errors, entail far smaller financial and technical risks, have shorter and more controllable execution times, and benefit far more from network economies as they are, generally, improvements on or additions to already existing action networks (Prud'homme, 2011). In other words, large infrastructure projects impact more forcefully on the diversified and already active world of the multiple actions of countless agents, while small-infrastructure projects fit more compatibly with it. This does not mean that we should never invest in large infrastructures; it means that we should be aware of the difficulties – and we should always consider alternative, small-scale solutions. As Hugo Priemus (2007: 627) has aptly pointed out: in the development of large infrastructure projects, too often the *solution* precedes the *problem*; in short, without taking the real, complex and dynamic world of action seriously.

Fourthly, priority should be given to infrastructure conceived not only for a single specific purpose (e.g. revitalising a Y-type economy in area Z), but capable of serving a plurality of different purposes – and possible to repurpose over time. Infrastructures, therefore, should be designed as means towards many ends. In this perspective, it is crucial to increase the adaptability of infrastructure systems and their resilience (Bertolini, 2007).

A fifth point is the need to provide also non-physical (public) infrastructures to facilitate urban action and interaction; for instance, digital infrastructures – public platforms, open data access sites, city dashboards, mobile applications, and so on – to connect and exchange with others. This aspect is extensively treated in the literature on the *smart city*. In general terms, we can observe that digital platforms act as transaction intermediaries and facilitators, reducing certain costs and connecting people for mutual benefit (see, in particular, Kiesling, 2018). We can interpret them as "epistemic frameworks for decentralised coordination", able to activate dispersed information, provide access to and aggregation of dispersed practical knowledge, generate new knowledge within the interacting realm of the platform itself (Kiesling, 2018). Note, however, that maintaining the focus on *action* allows one appropriately to conceive digital infrastructures as mere tools for acting, as means towards many dynamic and evolving human ends, avoiding rigidly engineering drifts of the idea of smart city.[22] In other words, the only truly desirable smart city is one that will increase the options and the spaces of action and interaction: that is, the one creating the opportunity for *smarter citizens* (De Franco et al., 2023).[23]

4 Conclusion

In order to maintain the positive aspects of complex social-spatial systems and reduce the negative ones, planning should be radically transformed. Firstly, it is important to understand that planning can only intervene on the conditions of action, not directly on the actions themselves. Secondly, and accordingly, planning should be focused on ensuring the conditions that enable urban complex systems to emerge, and then to continually adapt and evolve without producing undesirable externalities.

Notes

1 For a specific discussion of the issue of urban adaptability in terms of choice/action, see Carter and Moroni (2022).
2 See also Knight (1982) and Barnett (1998). It is interesting to note that this point was perfectly clear already in Locke (1690/2002), book II, chap. 6, § 57.
3 With a specific focus on planning issues, see Salet (2002); Moroni (2010a); van Rijswick and Salet (2012).
4 The distinction between private and public spaces is based here on the ownership regime. We are obviously not claiming that ownership is "the whole story" but it is nevertheless a decisive factor; in fact, ownership determines the legitimate source and nature of control over specific spaces (Chiodelli and Moroni, 2014, 2015; Moroni and Chiodelli, 2014). In

particular, it can be observed that, when the public authority intervenes on land and buildings which it does not own, it cannot (and must not) do anything but define the margin of manoeuvre of (private) actions; when instead it intervenes on land and buildings of which it has ownership it can instead transform them and manage them directly (Slaev, 2017; Moroni, 2018; Moroni et al., 2020a, 2020b).

5 For instance, the issue of taxation of properties is not discussed here. We limit ourselves to pointing out interesting recent studies that reopen the debate on this topic in directions relevant also to the perspective taken here: Foldvary and Minola (2017); Moroni and Minola (2019); Minola et al. (2020).

6 For more on this, see Alfasi and Portugali (2007); Mehaffy (2008); Hakim (2014).

7 As Zywicki (1998: 147) writes: "Decentralised, complex systems require simple rules, which will allow individuals to focus on making the many other mutual adjustments which they must make in order for the system to function" By contrast, complicated rules tend to place the power of interpretation and coordination in the hands of people other than those more directly involved in the action and interaction (Epstein, 1995).

8 This is the opposite of orthodox (and still widely used) functional zoning that fixes a priori the uses of lands; that is, the specific possible actions in specific places. As Alfasi (2018: 390) observes, orthodox, strictly map-dependent planning instruments of this kind were meant "to enforce very specific predefined actions on obedient actors, but first, the case of urban planning is unsuited for pre-determined solutions and second, the involved parties are essentially disobedient; rather, they tend to be innovative and practical".

9 Note that formulating positive rules requires more knowledge than is needed to formulate negative rules. As Kasper and Streit (1998: 97) point out: those who prescribe the behaviour of actors have to be aware of the means at their disposal and of their abilities, as well as of the possible consequences of the prescribed behaviour. By contrast, those who merely rule out certain kinds of action, as is the case with negative rules, only need to know that certain behaviours are undesirable; the specific details of the behaviour, and the assessment of its effects, are left in this case to the actors themselves (Kasper and Streit, 1998: 97).

10 They are rules (preferably collected in an urban code rather than an orthodox land-use plan) of the kind: (i) "Every building modification or new building must, in whatever place, avoid generating the externalities H, J, and K"; (ii) "buildings of Type A must not be constructed within X meters of buildings of Type B"; (iii) "each new building must be distant at least 1/X of its height from the closest existing building", and so forth. These rules define (unacceptable) relationships among elements of the urban fabric and their use (Alfasi and Portugali, 2007). In this case, I cannot know in advance precisely what will happen to lot D that lies alongside my own plot E (e.g. what type of land use will take place, what activities will be there, how many inhabitants or employees will come). I can only know that on lot D (as on other plots of land in the city), regardless of the type of buildings that will be realised there, certain negative externalities are to be excluded (such as specific kinds of pollution, certain noise levels, etc.), as well as certain relations among buildings.

11 As O'Driscoll and Rizzo (1985: 85–86) write: "The plans of individual are in a pattern equilibrium if they are coordinated with respect to their typical features, even if their unique aspects fail to mesh [...]. There is an open-endedness to their plans that allows for spontaneity or novelty".

12 Among the first to use the term "several property" was Maine (1875). For the debate on this topic in the nineteenth century, see e.g. Lefevre (1880).

13 See also Barnett (1992 and 1997). And compare with Merrill (2012: 2081): "The first advantage of the property strategy derives from its reliance on decentralised management. The property strategy draws heavily on local knowledge about resources: where they are, what they are, what they are good for, and what sorts of practices or techniques will extract the most value from them. The aggregate of all local knowledge about resources greatly exceeds the knowledge that can be accumulated and meaningfully acted upon by any centralised institution, such as a strongman or a bureaucracy".

14 As happens in certain situations, for instance, in Italy, where the condominium is the only possibility for any residential aggregation (moreover, the rules of cohabitation for this case are already defined in advance by state laws in very detailed and specific terms). See Moroni (2014).

15 Certain (kinds of) policies are suggested here as examples; they are clearly not intended as exhaustive (other policies can be imagined). What is interesting to observe is how, in these cases, "the right to acquire property in the first place offers a new avenue for invoking the power of property for redistributive instead of just conservative ends" (Serkin, 2017: 297). See also Imbroscio (2013).

16 On the latter point, see also Ram and Smallbone (2002); Morrison et al. (2003); Bates and Robb (2013).

17 Habraken (2016: 63) observes that, in developing the public spaces of traditional cities, pre-twentieth century planners were generally more aware of certain possible counterproductive effects, such as safety and the costs of controlling them. The result was that squares and other public spaces were more calibrated and at the same time enlivened by intricate social interactions and complex networks. On the contrary, the emergence of a "no man's land" typical of contemporary urban periphery, in which action and interaction are largely discouraged, is the result of modernist planning ideas which have openly contrasted city life complexity (Chapter 5).

18 On this, see Van Nes (2008); Dovey and Wood (2015); Porqueddu (2018); Van Nes and Yamu (2021).

19 Typically, the *go/no-go* decision is not usually considered at all or is inexplicit (Priemus, 2007: 627).

20 An interesting perspective is offered by Bertaud (2018: 147–148), who suggests that the main role of planners should be not so much to regulate urban uses and densities in advance as to accompany emergent and self-coordinating urban dynamics with progressive adaptations and improvements of existing infrastructure (by mainly focusing on the reduction of the time spent travelling and the cost of transport).

21 On the problems created by large-scale infrastructural projects, see the seminal work by Flyvbjerg et al. (2003). They conducted an empirical investigation of 258 major transport infrastructure projects across 20 different nations with a total investment of 90 billion Euros. What they found

was quite striking: nine out of ten of these projects experienced significant cost overruns. These cost overruns were particularly pronounced in rail projects, with an average cost escalation of around 45%. Bridges and tunnels also experienced significant overruns, at around 34%, while roads were somewhat more contained, with overruns of about 20%.

22 On the "technocratic" and "dirigistic" risks connected with certain ideas of the smart city, see e.g. Kitchin (2014), Vanolo (2014), Calzada and Cobo (2015), Krivý (2018), Sadowski and Bendor (2019).

23 In this regard, it is important to stress the following: the new communication technologies will increase and facilitate connections and exchanges (both between the public administration and the plurality of citizens, and among citizens themselves); however, it is important not to delude oneself that they will lead to the transition from market activities, in a situation characterized by private property and scarcity, to post-scarcity collaborative or networked commons. As Knieps (2017: 125) aptly observes: "No matter the degree to which the collaborative commons idea succeeds, the primacy of a society based on market economics and private property […], and the concomitant voluntary coordination of consumption and production decisions via competition on markets, will continue to be indispensable […]. Indeed, the future role of markets shall increase within the smart cities of the future" (see also Kiesling, 2010 and 2018).

References

Alfasi, N. (2018). The coding turn in urban planning. *Planning Theory*, 17 (3): 375–395.

Alfasi, N., Portugali, J. (2007). Planning rules for a self-planned city. *Planning Theory*, 6 (2): 164–182.

Andersson, A.E., Andersson, D.E. (2017). *Time, Space and Capital*. Cheltenham: Edward Elgar.

Andersson, D.E., Moroni, S. (2014). *Cities and Private Planning: Property Rights, Entrepreneurship and Transaction Costs*. Cheltenham: Edward Elgar.

Barnett, R.E. (1992). The function of several property and freedom of contract. *Social Philosophy and Policy*, 9 (1): 62–94.

Barnett, R.E. (1997). Coping with partiality: Justice, the rule of law, and the role of lawyers. *Roger Williams University Law Review*, 3: 1–18.

Barnett, R.E. (1998). *The Structure of Liberty*. Oxford University Press: Oxford.

Bates, T., Robb, A. (2013). Greater access to capital is needed to unleash the local economic development potential of minority-owned businesses. *Economic Development Quarterly*, 27 (3): 250–259.

Bergevoet, T., Tuijl, M. (2016). *The Flexible City*. Rotterdam: Nai010 Publisher.

Bertaud, A. (2018). *Order without Design: How Markets Shape Cities*. Cambridge: The MIT Press.

Bertolini, L. (2007). Evolutionary urban transportation planning: An exploration. *Environment and Planning A*, 39: 1998–2019.

Boettke, P.J. (1990). The theory of spontaneous order and cultural evolution in the social theory of F.A. Hayek. *Cultural Dynamics*, 3 (1): 61–83.

Brunetta, G., Moroni, S. (2012). *Contractual Communities in the Self-Organising City.* Berlin: Springer.

Calzada, I., Cobo, C. (2015). Unplugging: Deconstructing the smart city. *Journal of Urban Technology*, 22 (1): 23–43.

Carmona, M., Tiesdell, S., Heath, T., Oc, T. (2010). *Public Places, Urban Spaces.* Amsterdam: Elsevier.

Carter, I., Moroni, S. (2022). Adaptive and anti-adaptive neighbourhoods: Investigating the relationship between individual choice and systemic adaptability. *Environment and Planning B*, 49 (2): 722–736.

Chiodelli, F., Moroni, S. (2014). Typology of spaces and topology of toleration. *Journal of Urban Affairs*, 36 (2): 167–181.

Chiodelli, F., Moroni, S. (2015). Do malls contribute to the privatisation of public space and the erosion of the public sphere? Reconsidering the role of shopping centres. *City, Culture and Society*, 6 (1): 35–42.

Cordato, R.E. (2004). Toward an Austrian theory of environmental economics. *Quarterly Journal of Austrian Economics*, 7: 3–16.

Cozzolino, S. (2019). The creative city: Reconsidering past and current approaches from the nomocratic perspective. In F. Calabrò, L. Della Spina, C. Bevilacqua (eds), *New Metropolitan Perspectives. Smart Innovation, Systems and Technologies.* Cham: Springer, 606–614.

Cozzolino, S., Polívka, J., Fox-Kämper, R., Reimer, M., Kummel, O. (2020). What is urban design? A proposal for a common understanding. *Journal of Urban Design*, 25 (1): 35–49.

De Franco, A., Moroni, S., De Lotto, R. (2023). Energy communities in a smart urban ecosystem. Institutional, Organizational, Psychological, Technological Issues. In M.M. Sokołowski, A. Visvizi (eds), *The Routledge Handbook of Energy Communities and Smart Cities.* London: Routledge, 13–25.

Dovey, K., Wood, S. (2015). Public/private urban interfaces. *Journal of Urbanism*, 8 (1): 1–16.

Epstein, R.A. (1995). *Simple Rules for a Complex World.* Cambridge, MA: Harvard University Press.

Flyvbjerg, B., Bruzelius, N., Rothengatter, W. (2003). *Megaprojects and Risk.* Cambridge: Cambridge University Press.

Foldvary, F., Minola, L.A. (2017). The taxation of land value as the means towards optimal urban development and the extirpation of excessive economic inequality. *Land Use Policy*, 69: 331–337.

Franck, K., Stevens, Q. (eds) (2006). *Loose Space: Possibility and Diversity in Urban Life.* London: Routledge.

Habraken, N.J. (1998). *The Structure of the Ordinary.* Cambridge, MA: The MIT Press .

Habraken, N.J. (2016). Cultivating complexity: The need for a shift in cognition. In J. Portugali, E. Stolk (eds), *Complexity, Cognition, Urban Planning and Design.* Berlin: Springer, 55–74.

Hakim, B.S. (2008). Mediterranean urban and building codes: Origins, content, impact, and lessons. *Urban Design International*, 13 (1): 21–40.

Hakim, B.S. (2014). *Mediterranean Urbanism*. Berlin: Springer.

Hamill, S.E. (2022). Restricting access to property: Citizens, owners, residents, and claims to property. *Common Law World Review*, 51 (1–2): 43–60.

Hayek, F.A. (1960). *The Constitution of Liberty*. Chicago: Chicago University Press.

Hayek, F.A. (1982). *Law, Legislation and Liberty*. London: Routledge.

Hayek, F.A. (1988). *The Fatal Conceit*. London: Routledge.

Hertzberger, H. (1991). *Lessons for Students in Architecture*. Rotterdam: 010 Publisher.

Holcombe, R.G. (2012). Planning and the invisible hand: Allies or adversaries? *Planning Theory*, 12 (2): 199–210.

Hospers, G.-J. (2003a). Creative cities: Breeding places in the knowledge economy. *Knowledge, Technology and Policy*, 16: 143–162.

Hospers, G.-J. (2003b). Creative cities in Europe: Urban competitiveness in the knowledge economy. *Intereconomics*, 38 (5): 260–269.

Imbroscio, D. (2013). From redistribution to ownership: Toward an alternative urban policy for America's cities. *Urban Affairs Review*, 49 (6): 787–820.

Jacobs, J. (1958). Downtown is for people. *Fortune*. Available at http://innovationecosystem.pbworks.com/w/file/fetch/63349251/DowntownisforPeople.pdf (accessed October 2023).

Jacobs, J. (1961). *The Death and Life of Great American Cities*. New York: Random House.

Jones, S.R. (2007). Supporting urban entrepreneurs: Law, policy, and the role of lawyers in small business development. *Western New England Law Review*, 30: 71–91.

Kasper, W., Streit, M.E. (1998). *Institutional Economics*. Cheltenham: Edward Elgar.

Kiesling, L. (2010). The knowledge problem, learning, and regulation: How regulation affects technological change in the electric power industry. *Studies in Emergent Order*, 3: 149–171.

Kiesling, L. (2018). Toward a market epstemology of the platform economy. In S. Horwitz (ed.), *Austrian Economics: The Next Generation*. Bingley: Emerald, 45–70.

Kitchin, R. (2014). The real-time city? Big data and smart urbanism. *GeoJournal*, 79 (1): 1–14.

Knieps, G. (2017). Internet of Things and the economics of smart sustainable cities. *Competition and Regulation in Network Industries*, 18 (1–2): 115–131.

Knight, F.A. (1982). *Freedom and Reform*. Indianapolis: Liberty Fund.

Krivý, M. (2018). Towards a critique of cybernetic urbanism: The smart city and the society of control. *Planning Theory*, 17 (1): 8–30.

Lefevre, G.S. (1880). *Freedom of Land*. London: MacMillan.

Leoni, B. (1961). *Freedom and the Law*. Princeton, NJ: Van Nostrand.

Lewin, R. (1993). *Complexity. Life at the Edge of Chaos*. London: Phoenix.

Lind, M. (2007). The smallholder society. *Harvard Law & Policy Review*, 1: 143–160.

Locke, J. (1690). *Two Treatises of Government*. London: J.M. Dent, 2002.
Maine, H.S. (1875). *Lectures on the Early History of Institutions*. London: John Murray.
Mehaffy, M.W. (2008). Generative methods in urban design: a progress assessment. *Journal of Urbanism*, 1 (1): 57–75.
Merrill, T.W. (2012). The property strategy. *University of Pennsylvania Law Review*, 160, 2061–2095.
Minola, L.A., Foldvary, F.E., Andersson, D.E. (2020). Fiscal principles for self-organising cities. *Environment and Planning B*, 47 (2): 235–250.
Moroni, S. (2010a). Rethinking the theory and practice of land-use regulation. Towards nomocracy. *Planning Theory*, 9 (2): 137–155.
Moroni, S. (2010b). An evolutionary theory of institutions and a dynamic approach to reform. *Planning Theory*, 9 (4): 275–297.
Moroni, S. (2011). Land-use regulation for the creative city. In D.E. Andersson, A.E. Andersson, C. Mellander (eds), *Handbook of Creative Cities*. Cheltenham: Edward Elgar, 343–364.
Moroni, S. (2014). Towards a general theory of contractual communities. In D.E. Andersson, S. Moroni (eds), *Cities and Private Planning*. Cheltenham: Edward Elgar, 38–65.
Moroni, S. (2015). Complexity and the inherent limits of explanation and prediction: Urban codes for self-organising cities. *Planning Theory*, 14 (3): 248–267.
Moroni, S. (2018). Planning, law, ownership: Hayek and beyond. *Planning Theory*, 17 (2): 305–310.
Moroni, S. (2023). Distinguishing 'planning' from the 'plan'. Institutional and professional implications of taking urban complexity seriously. *European Planning Studies*, 31 (11): 2327–2341.
Moroni, S., Buitelaar, E., Sorel, N., Cozzolino, S. (2018). Simple planning rules for complex urban problems. *Journal of Planning Education and Research*, 40 (3): 320–331.
Moroni, S., Chiffi, D. (2022). Uncertainty and planning: Cities, technologies and public decision-making. *Perspectives on Science*, 30 (2): 237–259.
Moroni, S., Chiodelli, F. (2014). Public spaces, private spaces, and the right to the city. *International Journal of E-Planning Research*, 3 (1): 51–65.
Moroni, S., De Franco, A., Bellè, B.M. (2020a). Vacant buildings. Distinguishing heterogeneous cases: Public items versus private items; empty properties versus abandoned properties. In I. Lami (ed.), *Abandoned Buildings in Contemporary cities: Smart Conditions for Actions*. Berlin: Springer, 9–18.
Moroni, S., De Franco, A., Bellè, B.M. (2020b). Unused private and public buildings: Re-discussing merely empty and truly abandoned situations, with particular reference to the case of Italy and the city of Milan. *Journal of Urban Affairs*, 42 (8): 1299–1320.
Moroni, S., Minola, L. (2019). Unnatural sprawl: Reconsidering public responsibility for suburban development in Italy, and the desirability and possibility of changing the rules of the game. *Land Use Policy*, 86: 104–112.

Morrison, A., Breen, J., Ali, S. (2003). Small business growth: intention, ability, and opportunity. *Journal of Small Business Management*, 41 (4): 417–425.

O'Driscoll, G.P., Rizzo, M.J. (1985). *The Economics of Time and Ignorance*. London: Routledge.

Ponti, M. (2007). *Una politica per i trasporti italiani*. Roma-Bari: Laterza.

Ponti, M. (2015). Il Principe, i trasporti. In M. Ponti, S. Moroni, F. Ramella (eds), *L'arbitrio del principe*. Torino: IBL, 35–92.

Ponti, M., Boitani, A., Ramella, F. (2013). The European transport policy: Its main issues. *Case Studies on Transport Policy*, 1 (1–2): 53–62.

Porqueddu, E. (2018). Toward the open city: Design and research for emergent urban systems. *Urban Design International*, 23: 236–248.

Priemus, H. (2007). Development and design of large infrastructure projects: Disregarded alternatives and issues of spatial planning. *Environment and Planning B*, 34: 626–644.

Priemus, H. (2010). Decision-making on mega-projects. *European Journal of Transport and Infrastructure Research*, 10 (1): 19–29.

Priemus, H. (2012). How to improve the early stages of decision-making on mega-projects. In H. Priemus, B. Flyvbjerg, B. van Wee (eds), *Decision-Making on Mega-Projects*. Cheltenham: Edward Elgar, 105–119.

Prud'homme, R. (2011). Gli investimenti per i trasporti: le cinque tentazioni della politica. In F. Ramella (ed.), *Trasporti e infrastrutture*. Torino: IBL, 45–61.

Ram, M., Smallbone, D. (2002). Ethnic minority business policy in the era of the Small Business Service. *Environment and Planning C*, 20 (2): 235–249.

Roggema, R. (2014). Towards enhanced resilience in city design: A proposition. *Land*, 3 (2): 448–460.

Sadowski, J., Bendor, R. (2019). Selling smartness: Corporate narratives and the smart city as a sociotechnical imaginary. *Science, Technology, & Human Values*, 44 (3): 540–563.

Salet, W. (2002). Evolving institutions: An international exploration into planning and law. *Journal of Planning Education and Research*, 22: 26–33.

Serkin, C. (2017). The missing rung: Challenging regulatory barriers to property acquisition. *Property Rights Conference Journal*, 6: 275–297.

Slaev, A.D. (2017). The relationship between planning and the market from the perspective of property rights theory: A transaction cost analysis. *Planning Theory*, 16 (4): 404–424.

Smith, R., Warfield, K. (2008). The creative city: A matter of values. In P. Cooke, L. Lazzaretti (eds), *Creative Cities, Cultural Clusters and Local Economic Development*. Cheltenham: Edward Elgar, 287–312.

Tamanaha, B.Z. (2006). *Law as a Means to an End*. Cambridge: Cambridge University Press.

van Nes A. (2008). Measuring the urban private-public interface. *WIT Transactions on Ecology and the Environment*, 117: 389–398.

van Nes, A., Yamu, C. (2021). Private and public space: Analysing spatial relationships between buildings and streets. In A. van Nes, C. Yamu (eds), *Introduction to Space Syntax in Urban Studies*. Berlin: Springer, 113–131.

Van Rijswick, M., Salet, W. (2012). Enabling the contextualization of legal rules in responsible strategies to climate change. *Ecology and Society*, 17 (2): 1–8.

Vanolo, A. (2014). Smartmentality: The smart city as disciplinary strategy. *Urban Studies*, 51 (5): 883–898.

Webster, C.J., Lai, L.W.C (2003). *Property Rights, Planning and Markets*. Cheltenham: Edward Elgar.

Zywicki, T.J. (1998). Epstein and Polanyi on simple rules, complex systems, and decentralisation. *Constitutional Political Economy*, 9 (2): 143–150.

8 Annex

A case study

1 Introduction

The literature offers many ideas about what a good city or neighbourhood should look like. A common belief is that master plans and detailed building regulations can directly create successful urban areas. This belief is frequently reflected in university faculties of planning and design, where students learn how to design large-scale interventions but seldom study the characteristics of the urban areas that people prefer. For instance, when considering cities like Venice or Amsterdam, many observers focus on their physical shape and architectural appearance (Chapter 6). However, how many would be willing to investigate the codes and institutions that have made slow, open-ended, and incremental evolution in these places possible?[1]

As we have seen throughout the book, the problem with certain approaches to city planning and design is that many dynamic aspects of urban development, as well as people's preferences – especially over a long period of time – are beyond planners' control. In order to deal with this issue, an adequate plan should be able to accommodate long-term changes and processes that cannot be forecast once and forever at the beginning of the design phase. The main point is that planning and the continuous emergence of spontaneous social-spatial configurations should not be seen as dichotomous elements but as complementary ones.[2] In other words, a good plan should accept open-ended scenarios despite the problems and uncertainties that this might cause. As Jon Lang (2005: 367) writes: "An efficient design today may not be so in the future. The design goal is thus to allow for change, to create urban designs that are robust, whose parts are easy to change. Short-term inefficiencies may prove to be long-run efficiencies. Elements of urban form, buildings in particular, should be able to be adapted or removed with relative ease".

DOI: 10.4324/9781003454304-8

While an increasing number of studies suggest possible planning and design approaches to accommodate long-term urban flexibility, there is a shortage of ones analysing the formation and evolution of ordinary places and what planning measures have ensured their success.[3] This Annex carefully considers this issue. It investigates the design and evolution of Kreuzviertel in Dortmund – a highly appreciated neighbourhood often indicated as a "place to be" by many Dortmunders. It suggests that valuable insights can be gained by studying how the city areas that people like and appreciate have emerged and formed over time, and by focusing on the design framework that enabled their long-term formation processes and the real role played by planners in their success.

This Annex first analyses the genesis of Kreuzviertel and its main contemporary planning characteristics (i.e. those socio-spatial aspects that typically fall within the purview of planning). It then discusses the neighbourhood's most appreciated features and the effective contribution made by planning and design measures to their formation. The Annex concludes with some reflections on the effective role of planning and its interrelation with unpredictable emergent phenomena.

As regards the methodology used for the analysis reported in this Annex, it moved through five steps. The first involved the area selection and the collection of primary data and sources. The choice of neighbourhood boundaries was inspired by Barrenbrügge's book *Das Dortmunder Kreuzviertel* (2006) and Lynch's concepts of *edges* and *districts* (Lynch, 1960). To proceed with the analysis, blocks included in the area were codified (Figure 8.2a) and historical maps and the primary regulative instruments that had shaped the development of the neighbourhood were collected from the Dortmund City Archive.

The second step involved analysis of the neighbourhood's incremental formation by comparing several historical maps. Moreover, several items of information were collected by means of a literature review based on different sources and documents. Barrenbrügge (2006) and Hnilica (2016) were of great help in this regard.

The third step consisted of synchronic analysis of Kreuzviertel's main planning characteristics. Part of the analysis was limited within the neighbourhood's boundaries, while other findings resulted from comparisons of Kreuzviertel with its surrounding area (radius 1.5km; Figure 8.1a). The analyses were conducted using the Geomonitoring Information System (GIS) and partially with direct observation methods.

The fourth step was analysis of the area's most appreciated aspects based on the selection of fifty online sources such as blogs, local guides, books, magazines, videos, newspapers, podcasts, and real estate websites describing Kreuzviertel (Table 8.1).

The last step involved assessment of the role of planning in the generation of those aspects appreciated in Kreuzviertel: that is, evaluation of the planning choices that had contributed to the contemporary appreciation of the area.

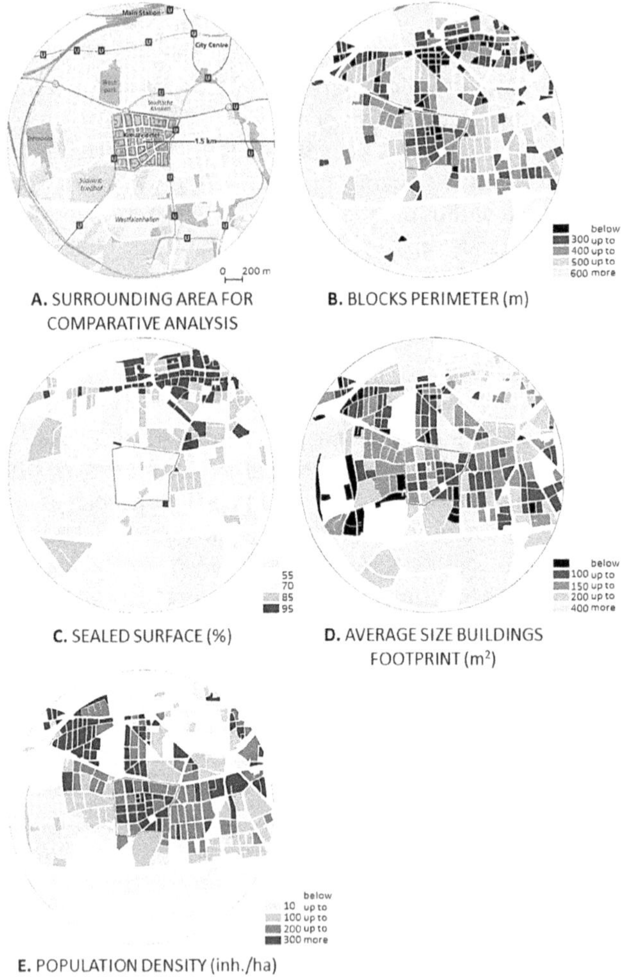

Figure 8.1 Planning characteristics of Kreuzviertel and comparisons with surrounding areas

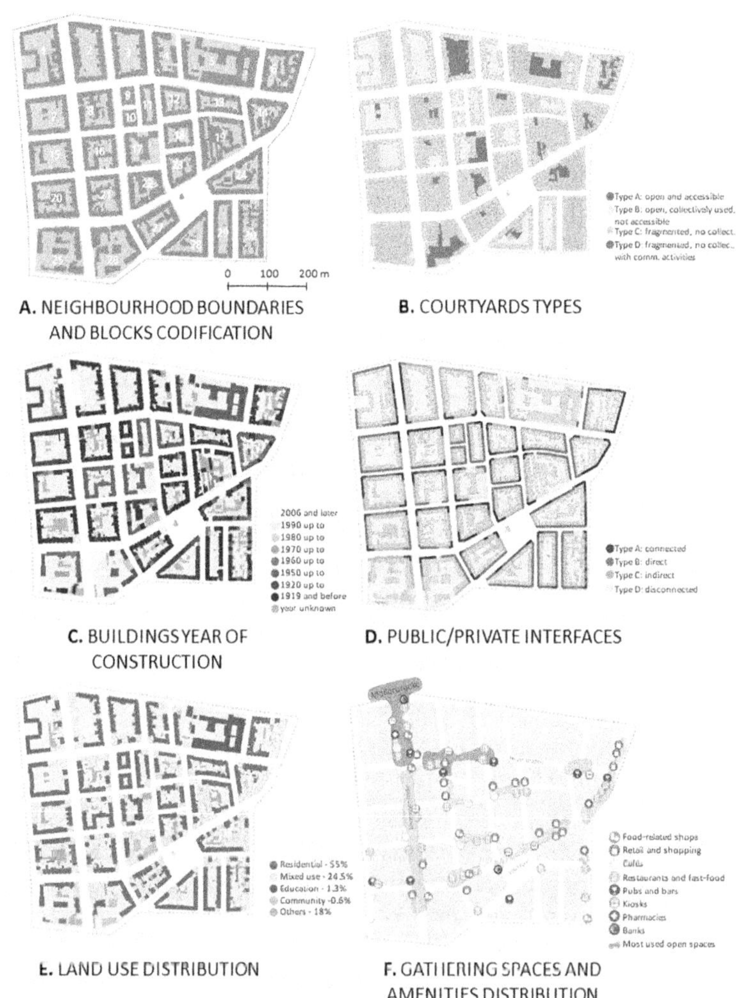

Figure 8.2 Planning characteristics of Kreuzviertel

2 Focus: The case study

In this section, we first present the design and evolution of Kreuzviertel; then we look at its major planning characteristics; finally, we explain what people like about this neighbourhood.

2.1 Design and evolution of Kreuzviertel

Dortmund is one of the principal cities of the Ruhr area, a northwest German region that became a major industrial centre for coal and steel production during the nineteenth century. A small town before the industrialisation period, Dortmund quickly expanded into a modern city, with its population rising from 44,400 inhabitants in 1871 to 142,700 in 1900 and 542,200 in 1939. The city, which currently counts about 588,000 inhabitants, owes most of its expansion to this historical period (ca. 1870–1940). Other crucial characteristics of Dortmund are attributable to its reconstruction after the Second World War and then its deindustrialisation (ca. 1970/1980) with the consequent economic stagnation and slow, and still ongoing, development.

The evolution of Kreuzviertel is distinguished here according to five phases: (i) the pre-development expansion plan (before 1898); (ii) the housing boom (1898–1913); (iii) the interwar period (1914–1945); (iv) postwar reconstruction (1946–1970); (v) neighbourhood consolidation (from 1970 until today).

Phase 1: Pre-development expansion plan (before 1898)

The origin of Kreuzviertel dates back to the development expansion plan of 1898. However, its urbanisation process started in 1848 with the construction of a railway and, later on, the station of Dortmund-South (future Stadthaus) in 1874. Due to the city's rapid expansion, in 1893, the municipality built Südwestfriedhof, a new cemetery just south of Kreuzviertel, and with it came Große Heimstraße (Barrenbrügge, 2006: 44). At that time, the Kreuzviertel area was almost empty, except for a few structures that would play a fundamental role in determining the further development of the neighbourhood: among them, the Neuer Graben canal, which traverses the area, and a few streets; specifically, Hohe Straße (the main gateway to the city), Kreuzstraße (which cuts diagonally across the neighbourhood), Sonnenstraße (a street running along the railway in the northern part of the neighbourhood), and the newly-built Große Heimstraße, which represents the western boundary of the area under study.

As visible on the maps (Figure 8.4b and c), only a few buildings were present in the area at that time, and they were mainly located along Hohe Straße and Kreuzstraße. This first phase ended with the construction of the Agricultural School (1895) and the School of Mechanical Engineering (1897) in Sonnenstraße. This intervention would have a significant influence on the area's contemporary universitarian character.

Phase 2: The housing boom (1898–1913)

The earliest design concept for the development of Kreuzviertel was formalised in 1898 (Figure 8.4d). It featured a large triangular square in its centre and several diagonal streets connecting with it to form relatively large plots.[4] However, the original design was not implemented due to resistance raised by the local landowners, who preferred a more regular layout more closely aligned with their existing property boundaries (Barrenbrügge, 2006: 47). To accommodate the landowners' demands, the city engaged in negotiations and redesigned a more regular street grid (Figure 8.4e). A land-coupling process was also implemented in order to reorganise existing land parcels and prepare them for individual development (Barrenbrügge, 2006: 41). The final development scheme resulted from both the landowners' reluctance to allocate a large amount of land for public use and the municipality's inability to support expropriation costs financially (Hnilica, 2016).

As apparent in the 1898 and 1902 maps (Figure 8.4), certain already-existing urban structures influenced the development process. Among them, Kreuzstraße (which, with the new plan, gained greater importance), the Neuer Graben canal, which was then converted into the main artery of the neighbourhood, and the two north-south streets, Hohe Straße and Große Heimstraße. Interestingly, the Schillingstraße of today exhibits a slight curvature in both development plan versions. This choice was dictated by the presence of an old factory (Figure 8.4d and e). To this day, Schillingstraße is the only "irregular" street in the neighbourhood.

Streets in the neighbourhood started to be paved and illuminated only in 1910. Most of them remained unfinished until most of the buildings had been completed. The construction of buildings proceeded incrementally from east to west (Figure 8.4). According to Sonja Hnilica (2016), the city had no real control over the private construction process. However, the *Dortmunder Bürgerbuch* (Dortmund Citizen's Book), published in 1898, set out principles that regulated the construction of buildings. These rules were not particularly intrusive in architectural and functional choices. Besides stipulating procedures for obtaining a building permit, they dealt mainly with aspects such as street alignment, guidelines for design of facades, safety issues (i.e. fire, gas, and how to treat wooden structures), nuisances (i.e. smell, noise, vibration), building heights and distances, and maximum building area.[5] These rules were mainly general (i.e. equally applicable to the entire municipal area) and negative (establishing mainly what to avoid and prevent).

A crucial aspect of the *Dortmunder Bürgerbuch*, which would impact the future of Kreuzviertel, was the introduction of a legal distinction among three main zones in the city: (i) the historic city centre, (ii) areas for expansion with no industry, and (iii) areas for expansion with industry. Following this distinction, in 1907 the *Stadtplan* declared Kreuzviertel a factory-free area (Barrenbrügge, 2006: 46). This choice determined a regime of exclusivity compared to the northern part of the city, which developed a more productive vocation (Hnilica, 2016: 46). This initiative contributed to differentiating between the different development processes and reputations of the southern and northern parts of the city, with Nordstadt restricted to being a place for workers and immigrants.[6]

In this phase, the street-grid plan was adjusted to meet new needs. For example, in 1904, the municipality created Vinckeplatz, a public green square which was not included in the initial development plan. Another change concerned the creation of additional streets because landowners considered some blocks too large (e.g. blocks 9, 10 and 11 on Figure 8.2a; Barrenbrügge, 2006: 51).

Kreuzviertel experienced the fastest development rate in this phase, with most of the blocks being developed or initiated by 1914 (Figure 8.4). In parallel to the development of residential buildings, new schools (e.g. Köngliches Gymnasium, Overberg, Pestalozzi and an infant school) and a neighbourhood church (Kreuzkirche) were built as well. With the progressive development of the neighbourhood, in 1912 the nearby old cemetery was converted into a public park named Westpark.

Phase 3: Between the two World Wars (1914–1945)

With the beginning of the First World War, the construction pace decreased substantially (Barrenbrügge, 2006: 101). This was due to a lesser availability of land – most of the plots had already been developed – and the war's economic and social impact. Between 1914–1920 there was less building activity by private developers, while there were some initiatives by non-profit-housing associations (Barrenbrügge, 2006: 103). In 1923, construction activity resumed, with new private initiatives and several public interventions. For example, the municipality created allotment gardens and developed three new tramlines connecting the area to Südwestfriedhof, Barop and Hombruch (Barrenbrügge, 2006: 106). In 1927, important sports facilities were constructed near the neighbourhood, such as a public swimming pool (Freibad Volkspark) and the Rote Erde stadium (today's Signal Iduna, the home of Borussia Dortmund).

The erection of public buildings continued with the construction of new administrative offices, schools and churches. The main idea was to cluster some significant public functions in the area (Barrenbrügge, 2006:134). By 1934 (Figure 8.4h), most of the neighbourhood was built up except for a few empty lots.

Phase 4: The reconstruction (1946–1970)

The disastrous effects of the Second World War were particularly visible in Dortmund, with about 66% of the built environment seriously damaged or demolished by bombs (Schildt, 2007; Figure 8.4i). Notably, a bombing raid in March 1945 almost completely destroyed the historic city centre, which was later rebuilt in the car-oriented modernist style typical of the 1950s. As for the rest of the city, Kreuzviertel suffered from war damage, but less than the city centre (Barrenbrügge, 2006: 167). Although the demolished buildings in Kreuzviertel were often substituted with modernist architecture, unlike the city centre, the overall morphological scheme of the neighbourhood was kept unchanged.

After the Second World War, investments restarted with strategic public interventions. For example, the municipality built a new school in Liebigstraße, rebuilt the one in Lindemannstraße, and reconstructed St. Nicolai Kirche and Kreuzkirche (Barrenbrügge, 2006: 180–181). By the end of this phase (1970), almost all the damage to private buildings had been repaired, with several new buildings built anew on empty lots. The reconstruction of the demolished buildings took time because construction materials were hard to find and often unavailable for private initiatives (Barrenbrügge, 2006:168).

Phase 5: Neighbourhood consolidation towards today's image (from 1970 until today)

In the 1970s, Kreuzviertel received an influx of younger people and was characterised by a "progressive" (political) connotation that was important in addressing future neighbourhood policies (e.g. introducing measures for the preservation of historic buildings; Barrenbrügge, 2006: 200–201).

In the 1980s, the area experienced the opening of larger supermarkets and a slow change in neighbourhood shops. In 1984, the Möllerbrücke station became the neighbourhood's principal transportation hub. In those years, diverse design concepts to favour pedestrians and cyclists were proposed, and some playgrounds were added to courtyards (Barrenbrügge, 2006:194). The 1990s saw an increase in international residents and a rise in the number of shops, restaurants and bars. The tram lines passing through the area were removed in 2002, and several bicycle parking stations were built across the neighbourhood. In 2005, the school in Lindemannstraße was demolished, and in 2006 the Fachhochschule moved to Sonnenstraße (Barrenbrügge, 2006:189–201).

Today, the area is celebrated for its historic character, and a good range of shops, bars and restaurants, and various initiatives aimed at improving its quality, especially for pedestrians and cyclists. It is largely frequented by young people.

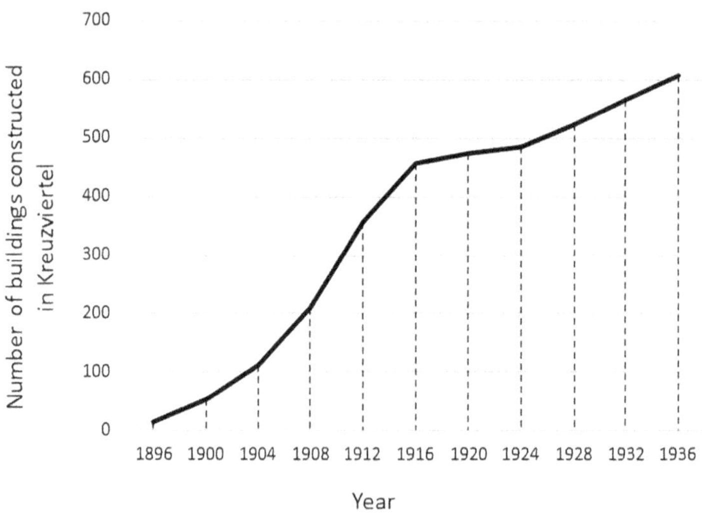

Figure 8.3 Building incremental evolution in Kreuzviertel. Data reworked from Barrenbrügge (2006: 64)

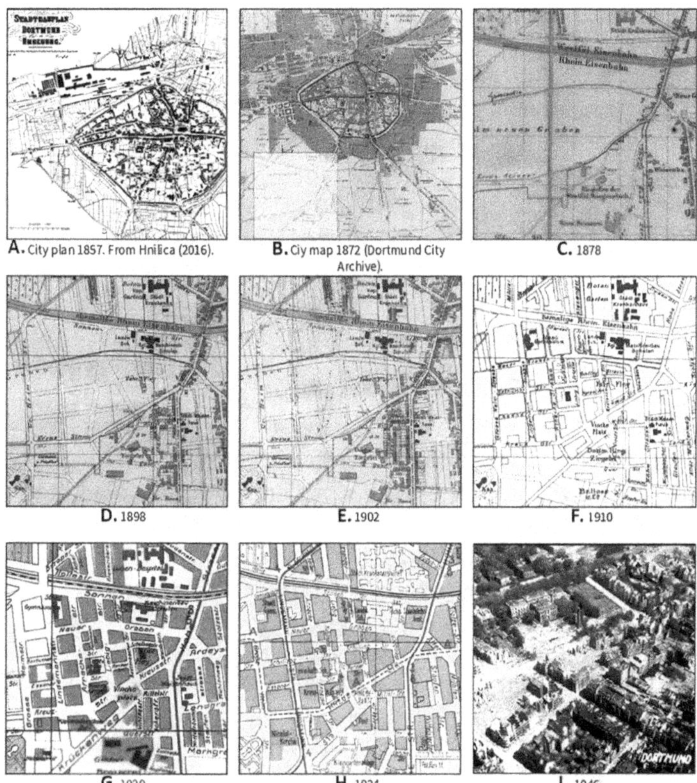

Figure 8.4 Historical evolution of Kreuzviertel (images b, c, d, e, f, g, h from Dortmund City Archive)

2.2 Contemporary characteristics of Kreuzviertel

Compared to its surrounding, Kreuzviertel has relatively small blocks, ranging from 0.2 to 2.2ha, with an average size of 0.9ha (Figure 8.1b). Besides block 5 (2.2ha), the large block of the Fachhochschule (the university building), all the others are smaller than 1.6ha, with 19 blocks out of 30 being less than 1ha. The shape of blocks is generally compact and regular, with edges less than 100 metres long (most ranging between 70 and 85 metres). This configuration generates a high level of permeability, that is, the presence of multiple street intersections which guarantees the existence of possible alternative walking routes and facilitates more interchanges between private and public spaces.

Kreuzviertel has an average of 72% sealed surfaces, ranging from 48% to 93%, with 16 blocks out of 30 with more than 70% (Figure 8.1c). Compared to its immediate surroundings, the neighbourhood has a large amount of sealed surface (which is, however, less than the city centre, where blocks reach peaks of 95%). Most of the land in the neighbourhood is built upon with only little room left for green spaces, which are usually located in courtyards or along streets, as in the case of flowerbeds and rows of trees. An exception is Vinckeplatz, a relatively green square that however plays a marginal role in the neighbourhood due to its location. The actual green area of the neighbourhood is concentrated in Westpark (ca. 9ha.), the former city cemetery turned into an urban park. Its importance exceeds the neighbourhood scale, with many people frequenting it for various purposes (see, e.g., Wilker and Gruehn, 2017).

An essential characteristic of the area is the presence of courtyards in each block (Figure 8.2b). Courtyards are of various kinds and have various uses (Table 8.2). Most are privately owned and used (23 out of 30). Of these, 12 are collectively used by their inhabitants but are not accessible by external visitors (type B), while 11 are privately used but fragmented into many small properties (type C). In total, only seven courtyards in the neighbourhood are publicly accessible; three are open for recreational purposes (e.g. public gardens; type A) and four for commercial uses (type D). Hence, the presence of courtyards, although it has different characteristics within the neighbourhood, is a typical feature of the area.

On average, buildings have footprints smaller than that of their surrounding area (Figure 8.1d). This contributes to greater diversity (e.g. architectural, functional, proprietary) and an overall "picturesque" character. Moreover, despite the bombings during the Second World War, a large proportion of the building stock dates to between 1890 and 1940, with only a small part being built after the Second World War (Figure 8.2c). Although the buildings constructed after 1950 have a different style, to be emphasised is that they have maintained almost the same footprint as those demolished during the war. The main difference concerns their architectural style. While pre-war buildings are rich with decorations in their facades, post-war ones are plain and simple.

The streets in the neighbourhood are mainly intimate, and their conformation does not favour car circulation (although the presence of cars is high in the area, with many of them parked on the street: Scheiner et al., 2020). An important aspect concerns the prevalent types of interface (Dovey and Wood, 2015) between buildings and streets (Figure 8.2d). Drawing inspiration from the work of Kim Dovey and Stephen Wood (2015), the three principal types in the area are: (i) *connected* (i.e. buildings with active ground floors for commercial uses directly accessible from sidewalks); (ii) *direct* (i.e. buildings without active ground floors or public functions but aligned to the street and in direct relation with sidewalks); and (iii) *indirect* (i.e. buildings are aligned to the street but physically separated by the presence of small green spaces). Finally, a small number of interfaces in the area are (iv) *disconnected* (i.e. a situation in which buildings are not connected and aligned with the street and are physically distant and separated from it). In short, Kreuzviertel is generally characterised by a close interrelation between buildings and streets which stimulates the active use of ground floors and sidewalks and, therefore, a vibrant street life.

Another characteristic of the area that contributes to public life and vibrancy is the presence of different functions (Figure 8.2e). While 55% of the buildings are fully residential, the remaining 45%, although primarily residential, present a wide range of uses. The retail outlets are uniformly distributed within the area, with a higher concentration along Lindemannstraße, Neuer Graben and Kreuzstraße. An interesting aspect is that some popular bars, café and restaurants are not located on the main streets but in the very heart of the neighbourhood (Figure 8.2f). This characteristic constantly attracts visitors into the area.

Lastly, an important feature is a high concentration of residents in the area (Figure 8.1e). Despite its mixed-used vocation, Kreuzviertel is a prevalently residential area. This aspect guarantees a constant presence of people in the neighbourhood. Unlike Dortmund's city centre, which is almost exclusively commercial and retail-oriented (most of the blocks in the city centre have fewer than ten residents per hectare) or other nearby lower-density residential areas (usually with a local population ranging from 100 or 200 inhabitants per hectare), Kreuzviertel has a population density that, in most of its blocks, exceeds 300 inhabitants per hectare.

2.3 What people like about Kreuzviertel

This section focuses on what makes Kreuzviertel "a place to be" (in Dortmund, at least). We analysed fifty online sources describing the area (Table 8.1). The result was a collection of 320 aspects relevant to the description of the neighbourhood, which were grouped for similarities into six main categories. These are now ranked in terms of their intensity/recurrence: (i) quality of life and culture, (ii) economic activities and amenities, (iii) built environment, (iv) population, (v) transport and accessibility, (vi) real estate value.[7]

The most recurrent aspect concerns the *quality of life* and *lifestyle/culture* of the area. This category comprises features contributing to the consolidated "trendy" image of the area, rich in leisure and recreational opportunities, but also offering a well-balanced combination of urban atmosphere and residential tranquillity. The mix of residential functions and a fine-grained mixed-used urban fabric is central in many descriptions of the area. This aspect is widely considered to be the main factor making the neighbourhood a desirable place to live. The area is also described as "peaceful", "colourful", "pulsating", and "vibrant"; offering a "village feeling" and a pleasant street life.

The second aspect regards the concentration of *economic activities and amenities* in the area. From the analysis emerges the appreciation for diverse gastronomic alternatives, multiple places (such as bars, pubs, and cafes) in which to "hang out" at different times of day, and a variety of small and independent stores combined with the presence of supermarkets for everyday shopping. It also emerges that other functions (e.g. the university or the nearby hospital, stadium and Dortmund Messe) give even more variety to the neighbourhood. A positive characteristic of the area is that it offers a nightlife scene more attractive than other areas of the city.

The third most recurrent aspect concerns the *built environment*. A salient feature is the presence of many restored old buildings with original and well-kept facades. Analysis shows the appreciation for the highly-decorated and colourful Wilhelmine and Art Nouveau buildings (which are not so easily findable in such a concentrated manner elsewhere in the city), combined with well-proportioned streets, most of them tree-lined and with broad sidewalks. The overall perception is that of a charming area which is also pedestrian- and bicycle-friendly. Besides the general characteristic of the urban fabric, Westpark is a major attraction factor.

Also evident in the various descriptions is the role played by the *type of population* living in the neighbourhood. The area is praised for having a mix of different generations and strong attachment to it by its inhabitants, which generates a "community feeling". The analysis shows that students, academics, freelancers, and artists/designers choose to live in the area. At the same time, the neighbourhood is also described as an attractive area for professionals from abroad, who find an international-friendly atmosphere in Kreuzviertel.

Another aspect contributing to the success of the area is its *level of accessibility,* which is due to the presence of multiple transportation modes and good connections with the surroundings. People appreciate Kreuzviertel's proximity to the city centre (15 minutes walking distance) and the Central Station (20 minutes walking distance). Also, given the presence of the Möllerbrücke S-Bahn and Kreuzstraße and Saarlandstraße U-Bahn, the area is presented as well-connected to the rest of the city and its region, so that non-residents can also easily reach the area to socialize.

Lastly, there is an aspect that sheds light on the quality and attractiveness of the neighbourhood but also raises some issues related to its exclusiveness. This aspect concerns its *real estate value.* Differently from the previous features, this one cannot be seen strictly as a "quality" or "reason why people like the area" but mainly as a consequence of it. The various sources analysed presented the area as "more expensive", "exclusive", and with fewer vacant houses compared to the general housing market of Dortmund.[8]

3 Discussion: To what extent did planning contribute to generating the current appreciated characteristics of the neighbourhood?

After presenting the salient aspects of the design and evolution of Kreuzviertel, its main planning characteristics, and the reasons why people like it, this section first highlights the positive impact of certain planning measures that have contributed, at least to date, to the neighbourhood's success. It then emphasises certain largely spontaneous and unpredictable dynamics that have also played an important role in the neighbourhood's current popularity.

3.1 Planning successful factors

Primarily, it is essential to acknowledge the crucial role of the initial planning framework, which facilitated and structured the area's long-term, largely emergent, and self-adaptive development.

Three key components underpinned the generative framework: (i) a robust *street layout* (designed in 1898 and adjusted in 1902 and 1904), which served as a physical guide for small private projects and ensured the presence of a dignified and indispensable collective space within the neighbourhood;[9] (ii) a simple *building code* introduced in 1898, which set out basic regulatory directives for private initiatives;[10] and (iii) the land readjustment that took place between 1898 and 1902, which reorganised and defined the *configuration of plots and parcels* and favoured a high degree of diversity by ensuring distributed design responsibility among several relatively small developers.[11]

The success of this design framework is rooted not only in its open-ended approach framed solely by certain structural conditions but also in some very concrete planning choices, such as: the high permeability of the urban fabric, which makes Kreuzviertel very walkable and dense (an aspect directly related to the presence of short-blocks); the prevailing typology of public/private interfaces and street alignment, which stimulates a continuous use of the public space; the possibility of having a dense and largely residential environment mixed with different functions; and the high accessibility of the area through various transportation modes (e.g., cars, trains, buses, metro) – which, however, has been implemented over time on the basis of different specific plans.

Another decisive aspect directly related to the design framework is the incremental nature of development. On the one hand, incrementality concerned the construction of private buildings over a relatively long period of time (ca. 1902–1934), which ensured the action of multiple small initiators. The main effects are visible in architectural variety (for example, in building facades) and in highly mixed and diverse plots. On the other hand, incrementality also concerned the various public planning interventions made in the area over time. In fact, the neighbourhood has benefited from continuous adjustments and projects by the municipality which has constantly improved the area by creating new functions and public spaces. For example, the decisions to locate certain primary, publicly important functions (e.g., university, Westpark, stadium, etc.) in Kreuzviertel and to develop strategic mobility nodes have positively influenced the neighbourhood and its surroundings.

One element that can be criticised from an ethical point of view but which has undoubtedly contributed to the area's positive reputation early on is its exclusivity regime established with the 1907 zoning plan. With this measure, the municipality has strongly characterised this area, and Dortmund South as a whole, by precluding the possibility of opening large new production sites, making Kreuzviertel more attractive for residential use. This contributed to a path-dependent disparity of treatment with respect to the northern part of the city that is still visible today.

Lastly, another important planning measure was the preservation act which introduced new regulations aimed at conserving Kreuzviertel's historic heritage. To be noted is that, in this case, according to the existing literature, the preservation act was connected to the presence of an active community committed to protecting certain distinctive features of the neighbourhood.

3.2 Successful aspects beyond planning

There follows a selection of dynamics beyond the direct control of planning that have contributed to the contemporary positive perception and success of Kreuzviertel.

The first aspect is the fortunate preservation of the neighbourhood's historic character. Compared to the city centre, Kreuzviertel was only marginally affected by the bombings of the Second World War. That unforeseeable event placed more importance on the neighbourhood's heritage. Moreover, the prioritisation of the rebuilding of the historic centre and the consequent difficulty of finding materials for the immediate reconstruction of private buildings in the area resulted in a slower redevelopment process which reproduced the already-existing morphology.

A second interesting aspect concerns the role of private developers during the housing boom phase (1898–1913). Although Kreuzviertel developed in parallel with other areas in the city with very similar street patterns, it attracted affluent developers who paid particular attention to constructing their buildings and facades. In other words, the same development plan could have had different types of builders with perhaps less interest in constructing quality buildings. In this regard, it can also be said that the prevalent architectural style of the area is another fortunate result. In fact, it is an incidental circumstance that today's society particularly appreciates the building style of that period.

Besides the architectural quality of buildings, it is also interesting that, in pursuit of greater profits, the various private agents involved in the initial urban development generated a morphological layout different from that of the original plan, with higher residential density, smaller plots, a more regular street grid, and less public space. Although this remains a hypothesis, if they had not pursued their own profit interests, Kreuzviertel would probably be less attractive today.

A third relevant aspect concerns several hardly controllable social dynamics that have made Kreuzviertel attractive today.[12]

Two of the most influential factors contributing to the current neighbourhood's success are "lifestyle/culture" and "type of population". Although certain urban policies may favour specific uses and/or attract certain people, the previous factors are, for obvious reasons, spontaneous. In short, who actually lives in the neighbourhood or uses the area, the type of social atmosphere, and people's lifestyle preferences are all aspects that cannot be directly determined by planning. The same applies to the kind of shops, bars, and private amenities in the neighbourhood. Their presence and distribution in the area result from a delicate and dynamic balance between market supply and demand that depends on the concrete choices of some entrepreneurs. In this case, planning may incentivise certain activities and businesses, prevent others from establishing themselves in the area, or limit their opening hours. However, their final configuration and distribution in the area are inexorably based on contextual market choices and opportunities. In short, a city is not like a large shopping mall or outlet mall that can choose which entrepreneurs should rent what, and what kind of businesses they should run (Moroni, 2014: 40–42); as we saw in Chapter 4, in a city this responsibility is often fragmented and dispersed among many actors, and it is difficult to centrally coordinate in detail.

Besides these relatively "fortunate" aspects, it should be emphasised that the contemporary urban imagery consolidated since Jane Jacobs' (1961) discussion of density, diversity, walkability, and urbanity – subsequently taken up by several authors[13] – as well as the current discourse on the 15-minute walkable city, well matches the characteristics of Kreuzviertel. Nevertheless, it should also be considered that the neighbourhood's success has not been sudden but has been gradually consolidated over time. This suggests that certain design characteristics are successful and remain important despite changes in social dynamics. Possible characteristics may be the open-ended and adaptable vocation of Kreuzviertel that has enabled it to accommodate various social changes over time (e.g. by adjusting certain uses/functions or replacing individual buildings), the presence of a variegated property situation that has ensured diversity within the area, as well as a wide polycentric distribution of design responsibilities, and an urban layout that facilitates and stimulates street life.

Finally to be mentioned is that, despite the strong morphological similarity between Kreuzviertel and other areas of Dortmund (Nordstadt, for example), it is usually preferred in the collective imagination, mainly for predominantly social reasons (e.g. street atmosphere and sense of safety). This comparison clearly demonstrates what was highlighted in Chapter 6: that the shape and form of the built environment is not the only factor contributing to the beauty and attractiveness of urban areas. In other words, certain social aspects, which are hardly difficult to control through planning and design, may play a primary role in people's preferences. This aspect is important because it does not prevent other areas in the city, perhaps ones with a less appealing built environment, from becoming more attractive sooner or later (for example, if Kreuzviertel becomes too exclusive and monotonous in terms of functions and population due to the continuous rise of real estate prices – a process that Jane Jacobs, in 1961, called *self-destruction of diversity*).

4 Conclusion

This Annex has presented a case study in which the importance of planning measures in the genesis of a neighbourhood, at least in its earliest stage of development, is relatively high. However, in reconstructing the formation, evolution and consolidation of Kreuzviertel, the study has shown that many important events and aspects, as well as the reasons why the neighbourhood is appreciated, are aspects that planners could hardly have directly governed.

A critical point emerging from the study is that the success of Kreuzviertel is contingent not only upon its physical form, although this is crucial, but also upon a multitude of social factors that cannot be directly planned (e.g. quality of life, type of population, economic activities, and amenities). Nevertheless, it is important to stress that, in addition to some specific public interventions and plans aimed at improving the neighbourhood over time, three framework planning measures have played a vital role in Kreuzviertel's long-term evolution and the accommodation of those aspects currently valued in the area, namely: (i) the design of the public layout, (ii) the building code, and (iii) the form and distribution of land ownership.

Although these factors are not always central to the discussion of what constitutes *good urban design*, the analysis has shown that, at least in this case study on Kreuzviertel, they played a significant structuring role. Therefore, one possible suggestion for those who intend to continue studying how to plan and design good neighbourhoods, bearing in mind their long-term and unpredictable development, is to take these three framework conditions into serious consideration.

Table 8.1 Sources and analysis of the area's most appreciated characteristics

Sources	*Built environment*	*Economic activities and amenities*	*Population*	*Quality of life and culture*	*Transport and accessibility*	*Real estate value*
www.ruhr-tourismus.de/de/themen/shopping/szeneviertel/kreuzviertel.html	///	///	//	///	/	
www.wa.de/nordrhein-westfalen/dortmund-nrw-bvb-westfalenpark-hauptbahnhof-einwohner-geschichte-sehenswuerdigkeiten-stadtteile-90006091.html		/	/	/		
https://visit.dortmund.de/kreuzviertel-dortmund/	//		/	///	/	/
www.ruhr24.de/dortmund/sind-dortmunds-szeneviertel-13156196.html	////	//	/	///	/	/
Osterhage & Thabe (2012)	/	//////	/	///		
https://brill.com/view/book/edcoll/9783846765289/BP000019.xml						//
www.ruhrnachrichten.de/dortmund-nordost/koennte-scharnhorst-ost-so-attraktiv-werden-wie-das-kreuzviertel-w1622705-p-2000213811/	//					
www.jetzt.de/atlas-dortmund/viertelkunde-dortmund-589849	//	//	//	/	/	/
www.ruhr24.de/dortmund/dortmund-neueroeffnung-kreuzviertel-kneipe-church-irish-pub-miners-corona-freitag-live-musik-2021-90980891.html				/		
www.ruhr24.de/dortmund/dortmund-kreuzviertel-moellerbruecke-sonnenplatz-umbau-plaene-szene-viertel-lindemannstrasse-rs1-90210395.html				/		
www.nordstadtblogger.de/500-ideen-von-dortmunder-buergerinnen-fuer-die-neugestaltung-von-sonnenplatz-und-moellerbruecke/	/					
www.nordstadtblogger.de/groesstes-wohnungsbauprojekt-in-der-innenstadt-von-dortmund-macht-das-beliebte-kreuzviertel-ab-2020-noch-attraktiver/	/			//		
www.muensterschezeitung.de/leben-und-erleben/ratgeber/karriere/studieren-in-nrw-munster-dortmund-und-bochum-1589295		/				
www.nordstadtblogger.de/dortmunder-kulturtipps-ausfluege-touren-ausstellungen-und-anderes/	///	/		/		

Sources	*Built environment*	*Economic activities and amenities*	*Population*	*Quality of life and culture*	*Transport and accessibility*	*Real estate value*
www.coolibri.de/magazin/orte-kreuzviertel-dortmund/		////		//		
www.vietze.de/kv-plan.htm	//	/	/			
www.aig-kreuzviertel.de/	///	///////	/	////		
www.youtube.com/watch?v=T[illegible]ak1jXHcVU			////	/////	/	/
www.youtube.com/watch?v=M[illegible]DKYKf5b7vg	///	////	/			/
www.hood.de/i/dortmund-kreuzviertel-ein-dorf-in-der-grossstadt-dvd-neu-ovp-eingeschweisst-80399981.htm	/		/	//		
https://visit.dortmund.de/szeneviertel-dortmund/	//	/		/		
https://docplayer.org/5614415-Schoenes-dortmund-warum-die-metropole-immer-beliebter-wird-januar-2015-feel-good-manager-wie-die-uniq-gmbh-ihre-mitarbeiter-begeistert.html	/	/				/
www.mpi-dortmund.mpg.de/studenten-postdocs/leben-in-dortmund		/	/			
www.leg-wohnen.de/immobilien/detail/9-128-M	/	/	/	/	////	
www.tu-dortmund.de/campus-wohnen/			/			
www.immonet.de/nordrhein-westfalen/dortmund-wohnung-mieten.html		//	/	/	/	
www.uskdo.de/2020/07/26/kreuzviertel/	/	/////		/		
www.dovoba.de/immobilien/immobilien-blog/2018/dortmund-seine-viertel.html	/	///		/	/	
www.wg-gesucht.de/artikel/dortmund-innenstadt-alles-wichtige-an-einem-ort-zentriert		/	/	/	//	
www.expedia.de/stories/ein-wochenende-in-dortmund-die-besten-tipps-fur-euren-kurzurlaub/	//	///		/		/
www.nrw-tourismus.de/dortmund#dortmunddirektundehrlich	/	///		/		

Sources	*Built environment*	*Economic activities and amenities*	*Population*	*Quality of life and culture*	*Transport and accessibility*	*Real estate value*
www.vonovia.de/de-de/wohnungen-in-dortmund	///	/////	/	////		/
https://lastjunkiesonearth.com/das-dortmunder-kreuzviertel-boheme-oder-bohei/	///	//	///	/	/	///
https://insiderei.com/listen/szeneviertel-in-nrw-koeln-aachen-dortmund-wuppertal-bielefeld/	/			///		
https://visit.dortmund.de/dortmund-architektur/	/			/		
https://visit.dortmund.de/dortmund-architektur/						
www.ruhr24.de/dortmund/unterwegs-kreuzviertel-soll-hype-quartier-13152914.html	/	//	///	////	/	//////
www.mein-ruhrgebiet.blog/perfekter-tag-in-dortmund/	/			//		
www.as-planenundbauen.de/wp-content/uploads/2013/09/AS_FourWindows_Broschuere_Korr.pdf	//	////		//	/	
www.ruhrbarone.de/wohnen-im-ruhrgebiet-das-kreuzviertel-in-dortmund/52560		////	//	/	/	//
www.dortmund-ahoi.de/dortmund/geschichten-aus-dortmund/dortmund-zum-hoeren-kreuzviertel-das-dorf-in-der-innenstadt/		//	///	////////		/
https://wuw-ibac.de/wp-content/uploads/Kreuzviertel_Expose_WuW.pdf	///	////	/	////	//	
www.bvbfanswelcome.de/das-kreuzviertel-hippes-ausgehquartier-und-bvb-epizentrum/	/	/		//		/
www.dortmund-ahoi.de/dortmund/geschichten-aus-dortmund/kreuzviertel-und-saarlandstrasse/	/	//	/	///		/
http://sight-running-nrw.de/karte/route/46	/		/	/		
www.immobilienscout24.de/wohnen/nordrhein-westfalen,dortmund,innenstadt.html	//		/		/	
www.ichwohnehier.com/blog/fotospots-dortmund/	//			/		
https://loop-redaktionsgruppe.de/Download/Dortmund_nix%20wie%20hin.pdf	//	///	///	////		

Table 8.2 Blocks' characteristics. Courtyard types: (a) open for recreational purposes; (b) private and collectively used by residents; (c) private and fragmented into many small properties/parcels; (d) open for commercial/productive uses

Block No.	*Block size (in ha)*	*No. Building*	*Av. Building-Size (in m²)*	*Sealed area (in %)*	*Type of courtyard*
1	1.6	44	162.2	56	B (C)
2	1.3	28	214.1	70	B
3	1.1	28	173.7	49	A
4	0.7	18	191.9	63	B
5	2.2	25	429.1	77	C (D)
6	1.0	47	133.9	73	D (B)
7	1.0	23	201.4	48	B
8	0.9	43	118.5	73	C (D)
9	0.2	7	189.7	76	B
10	0.2	5	247.2	82	B
11	0.4	13	197.2	93	B
12	0.5	23	133.2	81	C (D)
13	0.6	28	120.1	69	B (C)
14	0.8	47	101.9	89	C (D)
15	0.9	28	164.9	54	B (C)
16	0.8	30	137.8	74	C (D)
17	0.7	17	184.5	68	D (B)
18	0.5	24	119.5	79	B (C)
19	1.3	61	117.2	89	C (D)
20	1.1	43	147.3	66	C
21	0.9	37	137.0	68	C (D)
22	0.8	21	222.0	72	A (C)
23	0.6	33	108.4	70	C
24	1.1	52	124.8	80	C (D)
25	1.4	32	159.9	57	C
26	1.3	19	297.3	60	A (C)
27	0.8	43	106.3	90	C (D)
28	0.9	37	135.3	66	B (D)
29	0.7	33	120.0	67	B
30	0.9	66	78.7	81	C

Dortmund City Archive

1 200-01_0_0005. City planning map, 1872.
2 200-01_0_0010_1. City planning map, 1978.
3 200-01_0_0014-4. City planning map, 1898.
4 200-01_0_0016. City planning map, 1902.
5 200-01_0_0031. City planning map, 1910.
6 200-01_0_0048. City planning map, 1920.
7 200-01_0_0055. City planning map, 1934.
8 Dortmunder Bürgerbuch: Sammlung der Ortsstatuten, Polizei-Verordnungen, Regulative u.s.w. für die Stadt Dortmund, 1898 / (Dortmund citizen's book: collection of local statutes, police ordinances, regulations etc. for the city of Dortmund, 1898)

Notes

1 On this topic, see Vance (1990), Kostof (1991), Habraken (1998), Hakim (2008 and 2014), Romano (2008 and 2010), Slaev et al. (2022) and Thinh and Kamalipour (2022).
2 On this topic, see Moroni (2011, 2012), Holcombe (2012), Cozzolino et al. (2017), Ikeda (2017), Kamalipour and Dovey (2017), Bertaud (2018), Buitelaar et al. (2021), and Debray et al. (2023).
3 A particularly interesting work in this regard is Easterly et al. (2016). However, this study primarily focuses on the long-term evolution of the economic vocation and structure of an urban area rather than the planning conditions that facilitated them.
4 This design was typical of the urban expansion plans of that period in Germany; see Bentlin (2023).
5 In discussing the rules shaping the development of Berlin in the same historical period, Bentlin (2023: 51) states: "The instruments for regulating urban development were oriented toward fire safety standards imposed by building police, but not toward an ideal block […]".
6 Interesting works on this topic are Fischer-Krapohl (2013), Flacke et al. (2016), Hans and Hanhörster (2020), Wittowsky et al. (2020) and Shaev (2021).
7 As we will see, what is called "real estate value" here is a special category.
8 Dortmund is relatively cheaper and more affordable than other cities in Germany or the region. According to the website *ImmoScout24* (accessed March 2023), the average purchase prices of apartments in Dortmund is €2,519/m^2, compared with € 4,293/m^2 in Köln, €4,662/m^2 in Düsseldorf, € 4,040/m^2 in Münster, €2,576/m^2 in Essen, and €2,541/m^2 Bochum. However, within Dortmund, there are marked differences. For example, the average purchase price in Kreuzviertel is €3,849/m^2, while in the northern part of the city it is €2,307/m^2 in Hafen-Südost, and €1,635/m^2 in Nordmarkt-Südost. On this topic, see also Swanstrom and Plöger (2022).
9 On this topic, see Mouthing (1992), Salingaros (1998), and Porta and Romice (2014).

10 See e.g. Alfasi and Portugali (2007), Hakim (2008), and Talen (2012).
11 On this topic, see e.g. Bobkova et al. (2019).
12 On this topic, see Holcombe (2012) and Bertaud (2018).
13 See e.g. Sennett (1970), Jacobs and Appleyard (1987), Florida (2005) and Gehl (2010).

References

Alfasi, N., Portugali, J. (2007). Planning rules for a self-planned city, *Planning Theory*, 6 (2): 164–182.

Barrenbrügge, C. (2006). *Das Dortmunder Kreuzviertel*. Norderstedt: Books on Demand.

Bentlin, F. (2023). The urban expansion of Berlin, 1862–1900: Hobrecht's Plan, *Buildings and Cities*, 4 (1): 36–54.

Bertaud, A. (2018). *Order without Design. How Markets Shape Cities*. Cambridge, MA: The MIT Press.

Bobkova, E., Marcus, L., Berghauser Pont, M., Stavroulaki, I., Bolin, D. (2019). Structure of plot systems and economic activity in cities: Linking plot types to retail and food services in London, Amsterdam and Stockholm. *Urban Science*, 3 (3): 1–22.

Buitelaar, E., Moroni, S., De Franco, A. (2021). Building obsolescence in the evolving city. Reframing property vacancy and abandonment in the light of urban dynamics and complexity. *Cities*, 108: 1–7.

Cozzolino, S., Buitelaar, E., Moroni, S., Sorel, N. (2017). Experimenting in urban self-organization. Framework-rules and emerging orders in Oosterwold (Almere, The Netherlands). *Cosmos and Taxis*, 4 (2): 49–59.

Debray, H., Kraff, N.J., Zhu, X.X., Taubenböck, H. (2023). Planned, unplanned, or in-between? A concept of the intensity of plannedness and its empirical relation to the built urban landscape across the globe. *Landscape and Urban Planning*, 233: 1–27.

Dovey, K., Wood, S. (2015). Public/private urban interfaces: Type, adaptation, assemblage. *Journal of Urbanism*, 8 (1):1–16.

Easterly, W., Freschi, L., Pennings, S. (2016). *A long history of a short block: Four centuries of development surprises on a single stretch of a New York City Street*. DRI Working Paper no. 97. Available at www.nyudri.org/research-index/2016/greenestjune (Accessed June 2023).

Fischer-Krapohl, I. (2013). The Turkish migrant economy in Dortmund. An economy of urban diversity. In D. Reuschke, M. Salzbrunn, K. Schönhärl (eds), *The Economies of Urban Diversity: The Ruhr Area and Istanbul*. Berlin: Springer, 165–187.

Flacke, J., Schüle, S. A., Köckler, H., Bolte, G. (2016). Mapping environmental inequalities relevant for health for informing urban planning interventions. A case study in the city of Dortmund, Germany. *International Journal of Environmental Research and Public Health*, 13 (7): 1–19.

Florida, R.L. (2005). *Cities and the Creative Class*. London: Routledge.

Gehl, J. (2010). *Cities for People*. Washington, DC: Island Press.

Habraken, N.J. (1998). *The Structure of the Ordinary*. Cambridge, MA: The MIT Press.

Hakim, B.S. (2008). Mediterranean urban and building codes: Origins, content, impact, and lessons. *Urban Design International*, 13 (1): 21–40.

Hakim, B. (2014). *Mediterranean Urbanism*. Heidelberg: Springer.

Hans, N., Hanhörster, H. (2020). Accessing resources in arrival neighbourhoods: How foci-aided encounters offer resources to newcomers. *Urban Planning*, 5 (3): 78–88.

Hnilica, S. (2016). Die Großstadtwerdung Dortmunds und der Stadtbaurat Friedrich Kullrich. In M. Jager, W. Sonne (eds), *Großstadt gestalten. Stadtbaumeister an Rhein und Ruhr*, Berlin: DOM Publishers, 28–51.

Holcombe, R.G. (2012). Planning and the invisible hand: Allies or adversaries? *Planning Theory*, 12 (2): 199–210.

Ikeda, S. (2017). The city cannot be a work of art. *Cosmos+Taxis*, 4 (2): 79–86.

Jacobs, A., Appleyard, D. (1987). Toward an urban design manifesto. *Journal of the American Planning Association*, 53 (1): 112–120.

Jacobs, J. (1961). *The Death and Life of Great American Cities*. New York: Random House.

Lang, J. (2005). *Urban Design. A Typology of Procedures and Products*. Oxford: Architectural Press.

Lynch, K. (1960). *The Image of The City*. Cambridge, MA: The MIT Press.

Kamalipour, H., Dovey, K. (2017). Incremental urbanisms. In K. Dovey, E. Pafka, M. Ristic. (eds), *Mapping Urbanities*. London: Routledge, 249–267.

Kostof, S. (1991). *The City Shaped. Urban Patterns and Meanings Through History*. London: Thames & Hudson.

Moroni, S. (2011). Land-use regulation for the creative city. In D.E. Andersson, A.E. Andersson, C. Mellander (eds), *Handbook of Creative Cities*. Cheltenham: Edward Elgar, 343–364.

Moroni, S. (2012). Land-use planning and the question of unintended consequences. In D.E. Andersson (ed.), *The Spatial Market Process*. Bingley: Emerald, 265–288.

Moroni, S. (2014). Towards a general theory of contractual communities. In D.E. Andersson, S. Moroni (eds.), *Cities and Private Planning*. Cheltenham: Edward Elgar, 38–65.

Mouthing, C. (1992). *Urban Design: Street and Squares*. Oxford: Architectural Press.

Osterhage, F., Thabe, S. (2012). Das neue Dortmund Ansätze einer Reurbanisierung im Zuge des Strukturwandels. In K. Brake, G. Herfert (eds), *Reurbanisierung. Materialität und Diskurs in Deutschland*. Berlin: Springer, 287–303.

Porta, S., and Romice, O. (2014). Plot-based urbanism: Towards time-consciousness in place-making. In C. Mäckler, W. Sonne (eds), *Dortmunder Vorträge zur Stadtbaukunst* [Dortmunder Lectures on Civic Art]. Sulgen: Niggli, 82–111.

Romano, M. (2008). *La città come opera d'arte*. Torino: Einaudi.

Romano, M. (2010). *Ascesa e declino della città europea*. Milano: Cortina.

Salingaros, N.A. (1998). Theory of the urban web. *Journal of Urban Design*, 3 (1): 53–71.

Scheiner, J., Faust, N., Helmer, J., Straub, M., Holz-Rau, C. (2020). What's that garage for? Private parking and on-street parking in a high-density urban residential neighbourhood. *Journal of Transport Geography*, 85: 1–14.

Schildt, A. (2007). *Die Sozialgeschichte der Bundesrepublik Deutschland bis 1989/90*. Munchen: Oldenbourg.

Sennett, R. (1970). *The Uses of Disorder: Personal Identity and City Life*. New York: Knopf.

Shaev, B. (2021). A 'melting pot' city: Migration and municipality in the reconstruction of Dortmund. *Journal of Migration History*, 7 (3): 272–301.

Slaev, A.D., Cozzolino, S., Nozharova, B., Ilieva, J. (2022). The spontaneous rules of spontaneous development. *Environment and Planning B*, 49 (9): 2392–2408.

Swanstrom, T., Plöger, J. (2022). What to make of gentrification in older industrial cities? Comparing St. Louis (USA) and Dortmund (Germany). *Urban Affairs Review*, 58 (2): 526–562.

Talen, E. (2012). *City Rules. How Regulations Affect Urban Form*. Washington, DC: Island Press.

Thinh, N.K., Kamalipour, H. (2022). The morphogenesis of villages-in-the-city: Mapping incremental urbanism in Hanoi city. *Habitat International*, 130: 1–13.

Vance, J.E. Jr. (1990). *The Continuing City: Urban Morphology in Western Civilization*. Baltimore, MD: The John Hopkins University Press.

Wilker, J., Gruehn, D. (2017). The potential of contingent valuation for planning practice. The example of Dortmund Westpark. *Raumforsch Raumordn*, 75: 171–185.

Wittowsky, D., Hoekveld, J., Welsch, J., Steier, M. (2020). Residential housing prices: impact of housing characteristics, accessibility and neighbouring apartments–a case study of Dortmund, Germany. *Urban, Planning and Transport Research*, 8 (1): 44–70.

Index

For Product Safety Concerns and Information please contact our EU representative GPSR@taylorandfrancis.com
Taylor & Francis Verlag GmbH, Kaufingerstraße 24, 80331 München, Germany

www.ingramcontent.com/pod-product-compliance
Lightning Source LLC
LaVergne TN
LVHW010950110826
845149LV00015B/3290